The Billings Gazette

The Missoulian

The Montana Standard

The Billings Outpost

The Missoula Independent

The Independent Record

Left in the West

4 and 20 Blackbirds

Hip Hop Republicans

Organized by A.J.Otjen

With Edits by Jim DiPeso

2018

BILLINGS GAZETTE

Guest view: America of tomorrow will be 'none of the above'

Feb. 3, 2018 By A.J. OTJEN

For the last 150 years, Montana American Indians have experienced a wave of immigrants known as white men, the majority now. The U.S. Census Bureau projects that within 40 years, our majority population will not be white. Some believe this is because most of our new immigrants are people of color.

Thus, our immigration debate has morphed from the four pillars of the 2013 Marco Rubio proposal, emphasizing employment, education and employer responsibility. In April 2017, Arkansas' Tom Cotton and Georgia's David Perdue proposed legislation with a 50 percent reduction in annual immigration during the next 10 years, from 1,051,031 in 2015 to 539,958 in 2027.

At his State of the Union Address, Trump announced his new four pillars for debate. They include citizenship for "dreamers," border security, and ending diversity visas and family reunification. The emphasis is no longer employment status, it is skin color.

My family, Otjen, came from the Elbe-Weser Triangle or Lower Saxony area of what is now Germany. They settled in Wisconsin, currently represented by Speaker of the House Paul Ryan who is complicit with Trump's use of immigrants as political pawns. In 1905, Wisconsin was represented by my great uncle Republican Congressman Theobald Otjen, the son of immigrant Conrad Otjen.

Conrad arrived in the US in 1827 and became a citizen in 1836. John Otjen arrived in 1817, Harm in 1823, Hinrich in 1852 and Friedrich in 1854, all from the same immediate family. They were a chain being reunified from an area that at the time was rife with revolution and upheaval. They came to the promised home of the brave and free as part of what would be called the homeless tempest, an angry and violent world.

Their descendants include Major General John P. Otjen and William J. Otjen who was National Commander and Chief of Foreign War Veterans in 1932, my grandfather.

Every family from every immigrant should be as proud and welcome as mine. It appears, for example, that most of the Gianfortes arrived from Italy between 1862 and 1892, (likely the ancestors of Montana's Rep. Greg Gianforte).

Still, our Republican representatives seem to think that because most of us are no longer tired and poor, there is no more room for the wretched refuse; especially, if the teeming shores are on brown people countries.

They want to eliminate reunification even when the wait times for a spouse, child, brother or sister is as long as 15 to 20 years. About 225,000 immediate family-based visas are issued annually.

They want to eliminate the diversity lottery which accounts for about 50,000 immigrants. Using diversity as a criteria has made it possible for almost half of these visas to be given to immigrants from Africa, or what Trump referred to as "shithole countries."

They want to limit asylum cases entering the U.S. They cite children and families from Central America making up an increasing share of border apprehensions. The facts are about 25,000 people get asylum each year with the largest percentage being 30 percent from China and 12 percent from Egypt. About 5 percent are from south of the Mexican border. These are the huddled masses yearning to breathe free. No lamps will be lifted beside the golden $20 billion Trump wall.

On Dec. 17, 2017, Paul Ryan said, "This is going to be the new economic challenge for America, we need to have higher birth rates in this country ... we have a 90 percent increase in the retirement population of America but only a 19 percent increase in the working population . . . we need more people."

He added that he "did his part" with his children.

After not including credits for family leave or corporate day care in the new Republican tax plan, Ryan made sure the anti-abortion bill passed in time to brag about it at the anti-choice march on Jan. 19. He must not be including women in his working population. But he is counting on the number of new white babies to make up for a reduction in brown immigrants.

It's a fallacy. According to the U.S. Census Bureau, the dominant race in the future will be "none of the above." Our races will be diverse. They will be mixed. They will be American.

BILLINGS GAZETTE

Guest opinion: Paul Ryan leads, Ayn Rand rules

Dec. 23, 2017 By A.J. OTJEN

Paul Ryan spent the Bush years wanting large regressive tax reform because there were "makers" and "takers." He was touting the philosophy of Ayn Rand, with which he had fallen in love like so many of us did during our college rite of passage. He told The Weekly Standard, "I give out 'Atlas Shrugged' as Christmas presents, and I make all my interns read it."

Unfortunately, as the rest of us grew up, Paul Ryan became speaker of the House. He and his Republican colleagues passed a tax bill that will produce the largest redistribution of wealth from the bottom to the top in modern U.S. history, just as Ryan has proposed in budgets throughout his political career. Rep. Peter King, a Republican said of Ryan, "It's been his dream for 25 years before he even came to Congress."

Ryan believes that tax reform and reduced government spending is the key to enacting Ayn Rand's Objectivism, a philosophy of laissez-faire capitalism, the ideal economic system where everyone pursues their own self-interest. She did not believe in a public good.

Adam Smith, who is often misunderstood and misquoted, would not have agreed. Smith believed that government had a significant role in providing for a public good. He believed it was in our self-interests to take care of society. Ayn Rand, on the other hand, believed that any social contract was immoral, as it could only lead to oppressive bureaucracy and a culture that embraced mediocrity.

She wrote this in the decade following our nation winning World War II. Soon after we built a highway system, went to the moon, and continued to be the guiding light for liberal democracy throughout the world. Our investment in the public good and the resulting prosperity is evidence that Ayn Rand's philosophy was wrong.

In 2016, even Paul Ryan regretted using the terms "makers" and "takers", saying, "as I spent more time listening, and really learning the root causes of poverty, I realized that I was wrong. 'Takers' wasn't how to refer to a single mom stuck in a poverty trap, trying to take care of her family."

And yet, his life-long dream for tax and spending reform begins.

On one hand, Republicans have passed a tax bill that nonpartisan analysts say will increase the deficit by at least $1 trillion. On the other hand, Ryan said that congressional Republicans will aim next year to reduce spending on both federal health care and anti-poverty programs. He said during an appearance on Ross Kaminsky's talk radio show that he wants to reform Medicare saying "This has been my big thing for many, many years. I think it's the biggest entitlement we've got to reform."

Ryan plans massive cuts in order to pay for his new debt contribution. This is after decades of a decline in spending on what makes us a great nation: infrastructure, science and research, labor skills and education. Fareed Zakaria said on Sunday that we can't continue "coasting on past investment … we are ushering in a bleak future…expect big spending cuts on top of a dire situation."

Seventy years after her last novel, Ayn Rand dominates. "Who is John Galt?" no longer poses a literary mystery but instead symbolizes immoral taxes and spending at Tea Party meetings. There are 48 members of the Tea Party Caucus in the U.S. House. Our own Montana Tea Party calls itself Montana Shrugged.

These Republicans believing government to be an immoral collective that prevents the "makers" from becoming rich, are the same people who tout religion, fetuses, sexual behavior and skin color as moral controllers. They think they are Hank Reardon in "Atlas Shrugged", when the truth is they are Ellsworth Toohey in "Fountainhead". They protest and destroy government institutions while they stifle individual thinking, creating and learning outside the norm.

Ironically, our highways provided the very lucrative contract that started the Paul Ryan family fortune. Does he think his family's government contract was an immoral slope into the dystopia that Ayn Rand professed would result from public investment?

Yes, she wrote of a dystopia. Little did she know her philosophy, and Ryan's love of it, would make it happen.

A.J. Otjen has a Ph.D. in social sciences, with an emphasis in economics and political science. She teaches business courses at MSUB and lives in Laurel.

Guest opinion: Hope for Montana in November election results

Nov. 8, 2017 By A.J. OTJEN

The Nov. 7 election was a reckoning for Republicans nationally and in Montana.

Liberian refugee Wilmot Collins ousted four-term Helena Mayor Jim Smith, a known Republican who embraced the alt-right movement and rejected refugees in Montana.

Bill Cole easily beat Republican leader Jeff Essmann for Billings mayor. Essmann is a strict party-line conservative, denying climate change as an example. He also fought against mail-in voting, arguing it would disadvantage Republicans in the U.S. House of Representatives special election. He wrote, it "could be the death of our effort to make Montana a reliably Republican state."

When it comes to Republicans these days, Montana is rich with embarrassments.

Interior Secretary Ryan Zinke is now famous for spending tax payer money to scuba dive in the U.S. Virgin Islands and play with contributors in Las Vegas. He insists on a flag raising ceremony at the Interior Department when he is "in garrison." Instead of showing humility for service he displays a pomp of horseback and cowboy hat arrogance that can only be born from a well-connected Donald Jr. hunting party circumstance.

Senator Steve "What would Mitch Do" Daines had the potential to be a leader but instead fell in party line to be anti-science, anti-choice, and anti-environment, often holding phone-only town hall meetings where he does all the talking and none of the listening. He even uses the exact same talking point words as Majority Leader Mitch McConnell. He talks of "death spiral" Obamacare and "deeply disturbing and disqualifying" Alabama's Roy Moore. He is best known for telling Sen. Elizabeth Warren to "take a seat." And "yet she persisted." He used this moment to send a fundraising letter, proclaiming himself "courageous" as the acting Senate president with the power of the gavel in his hand for "standing up" to her.

Rep. Greg Gianforte is mostly known for assaulting the press or for being a significant funder of the creationist Dinosaur and Fossil Museum in Glendive, where man walks with dinosaurs on a 5,000-year-old Earth. He, along with the Laszloffy family, fund and lead the Montana Family Foundation, the extreme evangelical group that sends anti-choice and anti-gay emails to pastors asking their flock to vote for legislators who will take Montana back to the dark ages. They also push for school choice with the hidden agenda of teaching creationism as science.

The party that once stood for economic and environmental health and conservation has been distorted and divided with dog-whistle issues. More evidence of the divide is present in the 2018 U.S. Senate race. Former Trump adviser Steve Bannon has endorsed Matt Rosendale, but Interior Secretary Zinke supports Big Sky businessman Troy Downing. Retired Judge Russell Fagg is endorsed by former U.S. Rep. Denny Rehberg. It will be interesting to see these candidates take turns intentionally enraging the narrow, hateful base with issues as trivial as NFL knee-taking and gender bathrooms. Or they will try and control the vote. Republican Secretary of State Corey Stapleton has yet to prove his list of 360 fraudulent voters from 2016.

When Donald Trump took power, George W. Bush said he worried he was the "last Republican president." Maybe this is the last Republican grasp at power in Montana. The local victories of diversity, progress, conservation, science and equality give us hope.

A.J. Otjen, of Laurel, is a business professor at Montana State University Billings. She ran unsuccessfully in 2010 for the GOP nomination for U.S. representative and traces her Republican roots to her great uncle Theobald Otjen, Wisconsin congressman in 1895.

2016

Guest opinion: Political reckoning in looming death of GOP

Jun 13, 2016

By A.J. OTJEN

The Grand Old Party will die the same way it was born, over racism.

In 1850, the Whig party split over abolitionism and the smaller northern Republican Party stepped up against the expansion of slavery. Abraham Lincoln would be the candidate for president a decade later and win with 39 percent of the popular vote. That was 155 years ago. It is not the oldest Party in the country, as the Democratic Party traces its roots to Andrew Jackson in 1824 (i.e. the jackass). It will have out lasted the Whigs of 23 years, the Federalists of 32 years, and the Socialist Party of 71 years. Parties do not last forever.

As a fourth generation Republican, it breaks my heart to say the party is over. But my heart has been breaking for over a decade as the GOP has been sick ever since George W. Bush introduced his doctrine of pre-emptive strikes with the war in Iraq, leading America to lose our historic and beloved moral high ground in the world. In the last few years, the bitter taste of voting for

Republicans at any government level has left us starving. The GOP candidates that win primaries want to put creationism in the school curriculum, end safe and legal reproductive rights for women, and remove national parks and wilderness from federal management and give it to states without adequate funding or resources.

This is not good government. This is religious extremism or purity of principles with no practical application. This is party leadership pandering to an emotional voting base in order to win at all costs.

The final lethal injection happened last summer with the entrance of Donald Trump. A racist. Splitting this party as it began, over racism.

Trump asked for a "total and complete shutdown of Muslims entering the United States." When asked about the judge's rulings on the case for Trump University, he said: "He's a Mexican, I think that's why he's doing it. I'm building a wall. I'm trying to keep business out of Mexico."

No matter how they protest his statements, by endorsing him for the highest office of this country, both the speaker of the House and the Senate majority leader show that they actually do support his statements. These words guarantee the party's demise after November.

On Meet the Press on June 5, Mitch McConnell invoked Lincoln in defense of Trump when he said, "The party of Lincoln wants to win the White House, the right of center world needs to respect the fact that the primary voters have spoken ... we have a two-party system here."

Not for much longer. Would George H.W. Bush have wanted to win at any expense? Would Reagan? Not even Nixon agreed to a recount for the rigged election against Kennedy in 1960, as he thought the tumult would be bad for the country.

Republican leaders wanting to win at all costs are saying fascism is OK, as long as we get our socially conservative judges — judges that Reagan never would have appointed. Racism is OK, as long as we get our tax cuts — tax cuts that are ill conceived as they are already as low as Reagan and Kemp ever wanted them to be.

The GOP House and the Senate are also going to be lost in November. Because more than 30 percent of America is not white. Most of the 70 percent that is white is offended by racism, sexism and fascism.

The party of Reagan, Kemp, Teddy Roosevelt, Eisenhower, and Lincoln no longer exists. It has not been healthy for some time. Trump has killed it. He has taken a pillow of racism disguised as nationalism and snuffed out the last breath of the historical morality of the Republican Party.

A.J. Otjen is a business professor at Montana State University Billings and Republican precinct chair for Laurel. She traces her Republican roots to her great uncle Theobald Otjen, Wisconsin congressman in 1895.

Recent guest opinion worth a look

Jun 18, 2016

I hope people read the guest opinion by A.J. Otjen, a business professor at Montana State University-Billings and Republican precinct chair for Laurel, which appeared in the June 13 edition of The Billings Gazette.

She speaks eloquently of her concern that Donald Trump is destroying the Republican Party with his racist claims about Muslims and his assertion that the judge's rulings in the Trump University case are biased because of his Mexican heritage.

Otjen goes on to express her concern over the support of Trump by other Republican politicians. She is angry with George H.W. Bush's wanting to win in Iraq at any cost and with Republican politicians wanting a presidential victory without considering the fate of the Party. "Racism is OK as long as we get our tax cuts" and "the tax cuts are ill-conceived."

She rightly worries that the Republican majorities in the House and Senate will be lost as the Grand Old Party of Lincoln seems to have lost its way. I hope so: This Congress has delivered almost nothing of value; the bickering on both sides of the aisle is ridiculous and prevents important legislation from being passed.

If you missed the piece and know Otjen, I hope readers will send her a congratulatory note. Even though I am not a Republican, she expresses the concerns of all thinking Americans. Even my friends from other countries are afraid that we Americans have lost our minds and worry that American democracy is no longer relevant.

Dave Grimland

Columbus

BILLINGS GAZETTE

Guest opinion: GOP Congress can choose to govern or to fight Obama

Nov 6, 2014 By A.J. OTJEN

Both the U.S. Senate and House will be in the hands of Republicans starting in 2015. This could mean that there will be two early votes when Congress convenes in January. One to repeal Obamacare and one to do away with clean, healthy reproductive care for women. The president will veto both.

That could set a pattern for the next two years. The Republican Congress will vote for extremist legislation. The president will veto it. The discontent, dysfunction, and warring behavior by extreme personalities will be heightened because motives will be based on trying to win election in 2016.

There are two options for elected officials: Expend all their energy pointing fingers and posturing so that very little gets done. Prevent the other side from getting any credit for confronting important issues. Or share the credit for coming together for tax reform, infrastructure investment, sound energy policies, and immigration reform.

The Republicans could show that they can govern effectively in Congress. Or they can continue to get nothing done so they can blame everything on the Democrats, knowing that in 2016, the table is turned in terms of the vulnerability of open seats and the likelihood of a Democratic sweep is the same as the Republican sweep that just happened.

Republicans could find common ground and adopt centrist legislation, or they could waste their political capital. With every measurement of our economic trends showing growth and prosperity, will they reverse those trends with lower taxes and deregulation? Will they continue to push repealing Obamacare and for investigations into Benghazi. Will they prevent action on a minimum wage hike or equal pay for equal women? Will they push forward their "personhood" bill that no state has ever supported? Or will they give us good government?

Our elected Republican senator can be a positive influence by leading. He does not face another election for six years, so he can do what he truly thinks is right, not what he thinks might be politically fashionable.

Changing electorate

In six years, the electorate will likely be very different. The implacable laws of biology and our country's changing demographics will diminish the GOP's narrow base of angry white men over 60. Montana's population will become more diverse with the highest growth rates in Yellowstone County by far in the Native American and Hispanic populations, according to U.S. Census data. While the smallest growth rate in Yellowstone County is in the white population; and is actually shrinking for under age 20. The GOP cannot add to its base through subtraction.

Steve Daines is a businessman who understands that boosting revenues by depleting capital is not sound. He should know that aggressive extraction of finite energy resources will bring in revenues in the short term, but the long-term consequences could be dangerous for agriculture, tourism, hunting and fishing — all essential to "the last best place."

Montanans are far from the extremists caricatured in GOP television commercials. We are hunters, campers, fishermen, and farmers. We want our land and waters cared for and we want those who extract resources to take responsibility for cleaning up after themselves.

Hard fiscal choices

As a businessman, Daines should understand that shutting down the government or refusing to raise the debt ceiling are tantrums that reinforce public disdain for Congress, not sound policies for fixing the government's finances. Getting our fiscal house in order will require hard choices about spending reductions and revenue increases that will displease hardcore partisans. Someone in the GOP needs to tell the truth about fiscal responsibility, and it would be great if this honesty could come from Montana.

Daines can start now to get re-elected in six years by being a public leader instead of a party follower. He does not need to pander to a base in the party that he won't need and will be an even smaller share of the population than it is now.

More of the same is not good enough. If Daines does the honest and balanced job that true leadership requires, it will be a pleasure to support him in 2020.

A.J. Otjen of Laurel is Montana coordinator for Republicans for Environmental Responsibility. She is a professor of business at Montana State University Billings.

When dysfunctional politics get you down, think of the pets

Oct 13, 2014 by A.J. Otjen

It is very possible the U.S. Senate will soon be in the hands of Republicans, much like the dysfunctional House of Representatives. This means that there will be two first votes: one to repeal Obamacare and one to do away with healthy and clean reproductive care for women. Both will be vetoed by the president.

That will set a pattern for the next two years. There will be more discontent, more dysfunction and more warring behavior by extreme personalities. And in 2016, the Democrats will regain control.

We could worry about the Senate landing in the hands of Republicans. Or, instead of politics, we could think about pets.

My many pets have different personalities. We have hiked up mountain trails with horses and dogs with the same goal of reaching the top. Over the years, they have died of old age. In the past, when I lost a pet, it did not kill me emotionally. Because I always had others.

Lately, that "it-does-not-kill-me" philosophy is not working. Maybe it never did. I used to believe that it was nothing to jump onto a horse with the dogs and ride the trails in the mountains. Now, I look back on photos which remind me that it was not nothing, it was everything.

For a while, my dog Riley was the most loyal. He was a compass always pointing towards me. Before him, there had been Lady. I thought Lady was irreplaceable as my best friend. Lady and Riley were so well trained that I could take them to any café and they would quietly lie down under the table, not offending any of the other patrons.

When Lady died, Riley and I both lost our best friend, and became each other's. It was Riley that moved to Montana with me, and was not undaunted by a moose on the trail. When he struggled so hard on one mountain trail ride, I knew it was his last. Neither he nor the old horse with arthritis, Buckeye, would make it up the mountain again.

More dogs came. The dachshund EB refused to be left behind and rode with us on top of the horse in a saddlebag. A cattle dog, Patchie, loved every person who came along. She was like a ship looking for any port in a storm, attaching herself to every friend. "That's my dog," at least two friends said of her.

Then came a big Weimer (Rio) and another dachshund puppy, Otto. Everyone else is gone. Rio took his last trail ride two years ago. It's just to the barn and back for the old man. Won't be much longer.

As with Riley and Patchie, I will shake it off "because I have others."

Yet, I know that I am truly heartbroken over each and every one. I miss the dogs and horses getting along in the wilderness, even though they each had their own way of getting up the hill. Patchie walked right under Buckey's tail as Riley bounded back and forth over streams and rocky cliffs. Rio led the way with his bell ringing, always coming back to make sure we were not far behind.

Now, along with Rio and Otto, I have Beaufort and Moko, two big dogs I adopted because I want to again be that me on a horse in the photos. I want the sounds and smells, the breezes and even the moose. I want to ride the trails with everyone in tow, going towards the top.

But first, I have to get Beaufort to stop eating the remote controls.

Yes, there is a new horse and new dogs for this old girl. Each time these newbies seem too green to be on a trail, I remember Riley. The first time Riley saw a horse, he ran away as fast as he could, hid in a corner, and had a look in his eyes of "what is it?" But he learned. They all learn to get along and move up the mountain.

Yep, it's better to think about pets than politics.

A.J. Otjen ran as a GOP candidate for U.S. Congress in 2010 against Denny Rehberg. Otjen has been a professor of business at Montana State University-Billings for 11 years, and is currently the precinct chair for the GOP in Laurel.

Guest opinion: GOP must reclaim wisdom of TR, Lincoln

Jul 8, 2014 By A.J. OTJEN

Many Republicans have been waiting and wishing to vote for a Republican U.S. Senate. But no matter how decent or even reasonable Steve Daines may be, he is beholden to the party with a loud and demanding base that perverts reasonableness and insists on slavish obedience to a toxic orthodoxy.

Evidence of such is Daines' acceptance of the notion that government can dictate what we do with our bodies and what goes on in the privacy of our bedrooms. Daines says on his House website that he will "work passionately to promote a culture of life from conception to natural death, and protect marriage as between one man and one woman."

As a senator, he would have a vote in confirming nominees for Supreme Court justices. The base would demand that he only confirm justices who accept that regulating women's bodies is among the federal government's enumerated powers. One more justice in that corner and women will be forced to find coat hangers and dark alleys again.

Zinke changes position

If any thought there was any chance he would think differently on this issue, that possibility has been diminished with his co-sponsorship of H.R.1091 Life at Conception Act, a bill that would end women's choice as we know it.

As for our Republican candidate for the House, Ryan Zinke is walking down the same path. Zinke once was pro-choice, until the politicos convinced him he could only be elected if he checked the pro-life box on the litmus tests administered by the far right.

But it's not just these oppressive attitudes that make it impossible to vote Republican. Nationwide, the true believers in the party that gave America Abraham Lincoln and Theodore Roosevelt prostrate themselves at a pantheon of self-parodying crackpots. Ted Nugent. Sarah Palin. Rush Limbaugh. Anne Coulter, whose latest bulletin from the front is that kids playing soccer on Saturday afternoons are the minions of a diabolical left-wing conspiracy.

Daines dutifully worked on bills that satisfy the far right, make for snappy advertising slogans and have zero chance of enactment into law. If he is elected to the Senate, the balance of power in Washington could shift to Republicans in both houses. If you are aghast at the dysfunction in the House, as Speaker John Boehner has struggled with the GOP's jihad faction, imagine what would be in store if both houses of Congress fell to Republican control. And that is something for which most Montanans do not want to be responsible.

We could take a leaf from Mississippi's book. In Mississippi, the extremists lost. Senator Thad Cochran retained his position even though Ted Cruz, Sarah Palin and the Fox News arm wavers all anointed Chris McDaniel for greatness. And now, they are so outraged by McDaniel's loss, they are crying third party. If they leave, good riddance. Let them and their obtuse followers disappear into a third party bubble floating in a fantasy world of extremism and filled with the noxious gases of their turgid exhalations.

If Daines or Zinke want to be elected, they must not take their cues from the crackpots and crazies who have poisoned the Republican brand. Be real leaders and take the Republican Party back to sanity, back to the visionary leadership of Theodore Roosevelt, back to the wisdom of Abraham Lincoln.

A.J. Otjen is Montana coordinator for Republicans for Environmental Responsibility, GOP precinct chairwoman in Laurel, and professor of business at Montana State University Billings.

Lincoln and Roosevelt would be kicked out of the GOP

Jul 20, 2014

I read with much amusement A. J. Otjen's guest opinion in the July 8 Opinion page. In her editorial, Otjen advocated that the Republican Party return to the wisdom of Abraham Lincoln and Theodore Roosevelt. Not a bad idea, but while Otjen can appreciate that these two giants of American history were among the most progressive and forward-thinking statesmen in our history, I doubt their philosophies would play well with the current Republican establishment.

Both Roosevelt's and Lincoln's policies, with the possible exception of Roosevelt's tendency toward militarism in dealing with foreign affairs, would put them squarely in the liberal camp in today's political landscape. To think the ultra-conservative party that the GOP has become would accept them and their political philosophies is so far from reality that it's ludicrous.

Both Lincoln and Roosevelt would be run out of today's Republican establishment so fast it would make your head spin. In fact, Roosevelt was. After being denied the Republican presidential nomination in 1912, he left the party to form the Progressive "Bull Moose" party. As for Lincoln, I'm pretty sure he'd be appalled at today's reactionary Republican party.

And while I can appreciate Otjen's call for the GOP to return a more reasonable and middle-of-the-road stance, to go back to the policies of Roosevelt and Lincoln would put them somewhere in the middle of the Democratic party of today. Talk about wishful thinking.

Gerald R. Kessler   Billings

2014

 **BILLINGS GAZETTE**

Guest opinion: GOP campaigns ignore true meaning of conservatism

May 16, 2014 By A.J. OTJEN

Mail-in ballots are out and hundreds of thousands of dollars are being spent on advertising.

All the ads say the same things. Republicans continue to use dog whistles, trafficking in divisiveness that only the fanatical base can hear, to convince the few primary voters that they are the *most* conservative. They shoot the biggest guns, or hate Obama the most, or read their Bible more often than anyone else.

Their cartoonish sloganeering has nothing to do with conservatism and everything to do with playing crudely on people's fears. Yet they have nothing thoughtful to say about the most important issues our nation faces.

Threat to capitalism

Are they happy with the huge gap between the richest and the poorest among us? Conservatives used to believe in fair tax codes that benefited the middle class. Do they care that a shrinking middle class is the biggest threat to the future of capitalism?

Conservatives used to care about investing in big things for our future. What do they intend to do to re-educate our work force and rebuild our infrastructure so that we are once again the most productive and competitive country in the world?

Conservatives used to talk about our standing in the world in terms of manufacturing and innovation. Now they talk about it solely in terms of military strength, failing to understand, as actual military leaders do, that national strength does not lie in arms alone.

The Veterans Administration is in dire need of a re-invention, but the only word from the GOP Congress is Benghazi, Benghazi, and Benghazi.

Do they believe that global warming is a serious threat to our children's future? What do they intend to do about it? Are they recommending energy policies that will foster national strength, support our economy, and lower environmental risks? Have they given any thought to protecting

2

our nation's natural heritage and beauty? Conservatives used to be leaders in conservation. No longer.

Where do they stand on privacy in our bedrooms and our doctor's offices? Conservatives have always been the most concerned about keeping the government out of our personal lives.

Empty-calorie campaign

Do they really think that after a plethora of votes and a Supreme Court ruling upholding Obamacare that they can actually repeal it? And if they could, have they proposed anything of substance to fill out their slogan of "repeal and replace?"

Conservatives used to think that industry could partner with the government to provide the most efficient ways to serve our citizens. But not once have current Republicans offered any thoughtful ideas for repairing Obamacare.

Why are they not being real conservatives and offering realistic, market-based solutions that would not only fix health insurance, but purge our health care system of the gross inefficiencies and distortions that drive up costs.

We don't know. All we know is that they are tripping over each other on the way to a lucrative gig as another bloviating Fox News pundit.

In the Republican primary, there are four candidates for the House and three for the Senate, but which one cares more about the future of the nation? Which one puts country above party? Which one would we support in the general election in November?

We see a campaign made up of empty calories: gauzy ads showing one more walk in a field with the family, one more photo of the big elk they shot, one more mention of how many generations they have been in Montana. Because this is how we make our decisions on the future of our home, the future for our children.

Elections have consequences. Once again, we face the choice of sending a message that the GOP can continue indulging in dog whistles, or tell us who they really are and get back on track with taking care of the nation's business.

A.J. Otjen of Laurel is a GOP precinct chairwoman and an unsuccessful 2010 U.S. House candidate. She teaches business at Montana State University Billings.

Comments:

Run this woman for congress but her thoughts about what is best for this nation would never get her elected!

I am sorry that I have to agree. I have been a Republican most of my life, but in the past 5-10 years, I have found the Party seems to have no unifying philosophy other than "no".

As an old Monty Python fan, I am reminded of the "Argument Clinic" sketch, where the protagonist disagrees with every statement made by the other without offering any substantive alternative. As a result, I find myself voting for third party candidates, rather than "wasting" my vote, or choosing not to vote at all.

I'm still dumbfounded by the way those supposed conservatives treated the medical marijuana program. How is it not Communist to require a farmer to get paid ZERO for their work? They

Republicans need to see property rights go along with environmental development. I own property I don't want my groundwater poisoned.

Republicans care about their big oil money contributors, not the environment. We need more politicians who care about the country and a lot less that care about the perks their campaign contributors want from them. Politicians are destroying this country with their stupidity and self-centeredness.

Very good letter. My family was Republican, wanting less, more accountable government until they started trying to legislate Christian fundamentalist morality. Reagan started it when he promised assorted actions to get the right wing vote. Until they get out of my bedroom, stop attacking my LGBT friends and family and accept that women are able to make correct decisions concerning their own bodies and family, I will never trust them to make correct decisions about fiscal matters.

A. J.'s opinion piece is so accurately insightful and obviously heart felt. Good people, please understand that today's Republican Party is no longer the "Grand Old Party" which was begun by Abraham Lincoln and continued over the years by other great Americans from Calvin Coolidge and Herbert Hoover to the likes of Everett Dirkson and Bob Dole. The simple truth is that if the modern GOP does not divest itself of the extreme reactionaries, including the tea partiers, it will disappear and be replaced by a new group. The party of Abraham Lincoln began in exactly that way. I hope that any new party will be headed by responsible true conservatives like A. J. Otjen.

4

2012

Guest opinion: GOP must stop being the anti-party

December 05, 2012 By A.J. OTJEN

Will the GOP go back to living in the real world?

It can if it pours out the stale tea and reconnects with Americans where we are, not where Utopian radicals think we should be.

Tell Grover Norquist and other self-important demagogues with their narrow agendas to shove off.

Say goodbye to Rush Limbaugh and other media gasbags who breed fear and loathing for ratings.

<u>Rediscover Reagan</u>

Rediscover the wisdom of Ronald Reagan, Dwight Eisenhower, and Theodore Roosevelt. Go see the movie "Lincoln," and understand what Republican greatness looks like.

Pundits say Republicans have a demographic problem for the future, or that Mitt Romney was not the right presidential candidate. They're missing the broader point, which is Republicans have offended the majority of Americans with an outdated agenda that puts fear above hope, purity above pragmatism, and exclusion above welcoming.

The party seems determined to subtract its way to irrelevance. It has forgotten Reagan's maxim that the person with whom you agree on 80 percent of the issues is your 80 percent friend, not your 20 percent enemy.

Fortunately in Montana, the races for our statewide offices were not choices between crazy people. To be sure, Republicans lost partly because of issues as well as the likability factor. But we mainly lost because of the Legislature's extremism, which scared most of us into voting for veto power in the governor's chair. We also voted to make sure that the U.S. Senate remains outside the control of the sort of rigid ideologues who have made the U.S. House a byword for dysfunction.

The GOP needs an issues rethink. Here are some suggestions:

The GOP stands for liberty, and liberty is evolving to embrace same-sex marriage. Iowa, New Hampshire, Connecticut, Massachusetts and Vermont already permit gay marriage. Maine, Maryland, and our Northwest neighbor Washington State approved same-sex marriage by popular vote. Minnesota voters defeated a proposed constitutional amendment to ban same-sex marriage.

A party that says it wants government off our backs should also want to keep government out of our bedrooms.

Which brings us to the problem Republicans have connecting with women voters. Putting up ham-fisted candidates like Todd Akin and Richard Mourdock, with their medieval thinking about sexual violence, tells women that Republicans don't care about their concerns and don't think they need to care.

The results of that obtuseness were clear Nov. 6. Over 20 new representatives who have made women's rights a priority were elected. Roe v. Wade will not be overturned, and the only sensible thing for Republicans to do is to stop agitating the abortion issue and take up outgoing Indiana Gov. Mitch Daniels' recommendation to call a "truce" on social issues.

It's also time to revamp the party's thinking about immigration. As Florida Sen. Marco Rubio said recently, Hispanic voters have no interest in listening to Republican ideas about economics if they think Republicans want to deport their grandmothers.

We have the lowest income tax rate in history, yet economic weakness persists. Our biggest boom time was between 1945 and 1975 when the highest tax rate was in the 90 percent range.

Every time we have a large gap between the richest of the rich and the poorest of the poor, our economy has been brittle and vulnerable to recessions caused by a fall in aggregate demand. From the Gilded Age to now, the data showing the relationship between high income inequality and economic weakness is unquestionable.

Good stewardship

Finally, Republicans must reclaim the conservative ethic of good stewardship of our country's immense natural endowment. The technology exists to harvest our resources in a clean and sustainable way. We rightfully worry about the debt we are passing on to our children. We should also worry about the world they will inherit.

Republicans have to be on the right side of these issues going forward. We fail by being anti-gay, anti-choice, anti-working immigrants, anti-environment, anti-reasonable taxes. We are the anti-party. We must now be the for-party, one that offers hope for all people, not fear for some and disdain for the rest.

A.J. Otjen of Laurel teaches marketing courses at Montana State University Billings. She is Montana coordinator for Republicans for Environmental Protection and was an unsuccessful 2008 GOP candidate for the House seat held by Denny Rehberg.

Response printed on December 16, 2012

Thanks to A.J. Otjen and The Billings Gazette for her letter of Dec. 5. Please send this letter to GOP headquarters USA. Forget the idea of sending a copy to Rush Limbaugh. He wouldn't "get it."

America needs a healthy GOP party (maybe even a third party). I believe Speaker John Boehner is a good, thoughtful man but, wow, does he have a tough job!

C'mon all — let's work together for the good ol' USA. Forget the cliche of talking across the aisle. Let's really start something positive for all.

BILLINGS GAZETTE

Guest opinion: Montana GOP platform inspires hope for party's future

August 25, 2012 By A.J.OTJEN

Hooray, Montana Republicans!

The platform approved at the Montana State Republican Convention had two major changes worth shouting about. No longer does our party say that homosexuality is illegal. And, our party will work toward the legalization of medical marijuana.

One more change said the party wants local, state and federal taxes kept as low as possible. This is an important distinction from supporting the ill-advised Grover Norquist pledge in which lawmakers say they will never, ever vote to increase taxes.

I had planned to write an article about the dying Republican Party: That 50 percent of its members are over 60 and there are more men than women. That there are not that many minorities, gays or young people who identify with Republicans. Changing demographics and the laws of biology being what they are, a party that holds little appeal for the young and for minorities faces dismal prospects in the long term, which will be the short term before we know it.

But this new platform is a hopeful sign that issues important to broader constituencies are finally receiving due recognition.

I say "hopeful" because there is an election for our state Legislature this November. How do we make sure the Republicans whom we support agree with the changes and will actually follow through?

And how do we attract younger voters who support abortion, gay marriage or legalized drugs. They care about a clean environment and conservation. They are open to increases in tax revenues as part of a thoughtful fiscal package to balance the budget and provide the certainty businesses need to invest and grow the economy. They care about equal opportunity and economic opportunity, making them a perfect fit with the Republican Party.

Maybe, just maybe, the old guard running the party has wised up. Maybe the old guard has realized that if they want a strong party that changes with the times, that embraces the future, that is not afraid of diversity, and that wants all Americans to enjoy prosperous, secure lives, they will follow the new platform.

Our candidates can begin by refusing to sign all pledges, and instead promising to think through issues carefully and be willing to disagree with their fellow Republicans when their judgment dictates. Because leaders owe their constituents their best judgment, as the great conservative statesman Edmund Burke said long ago. They do not owe them total compliance to my-way-or-the-highway interest groups.

Our candidates should listen to Tea Party members but not be cowed by their angrier elements. Tea Party members are a part of the Republican coalition, but they do not hold a monopoly on the truth.

Our role as voters is to ask questions before we vote. Ask candidates if they will support the new platform. Ask them if they will stop signing pledges other than their oath of office, and tear up the pledges they signed in the past.

If they say no, then we should not vote for them.

This platform is the beginning. It is an important step in the right direction. And it should give all of us hope that we can make a difference.

A.J. Otjen of Laurel is a professor of marketing at Montana State University Billings and state coordinator of Republicans for Environmental Protection. She was an unsuccessful 2010 candidate for the U.S. House seat held by Denny Rehberg.

Guest opinion: Will 2012 bring the return of thinking Republicans?

April 14, 2012 By A.J. OTJEN

Republican politicians are fixated on culture wars.

New laws, or legislation now being considered, in the Republican controlled states of South Dakota, Virginia, Arizona, Minnesota, Indiana, Florida, Missouri, Kansas, Alabama, Idaho, and Georgia limit, restrict, or prevent women from obtaining various health services applicable to only females: contraception, mammograms, cancer screening, abortion counseling.

Before withdrawing from the presidential race on Tuesday, Rick Santorum had said that birth control is "a license to do things in a sexual realm that is counter to how things are supposed to be."

Is this an example of Republicans wanting to limit the size of government? This presidential candidate wanted to crawl into our beds and chaperone consenting adults. Sorry, Rick. You're not invited.

Both Santorum and Newt Gingrich indulged in theocratic presumptuousness, with bellowing commentary on the supposed religious errors of other political figures.

Santorum twisted John F. Kennedy's thoughtful 1960 speech about religious liberty into an attack on religion, saying he wanted to throw up. Gingrich accused President Obama of attacking Catholics and Mitt Romney of attacking Jews.

Wasted opportunities

By indulging in divisive culture wars, Republicans have squandered opportunities to offer a more inclusive, hopeful message about creating jobs and growing the economy. How many times have they promised to focus on jobs and the economy and yet the very first item on their agenda has been none of the above.

For the 2011 Congress, it was abortion. Five states with Republican legislatures, including Montana, have introduced legislation for a personhood amendment or other bills that would call into question the legality of birth control and raise the specter of government imposing an unenforceable ban on contraception. This, despite 78 percent of voting Republicans being pro-choice (www.gopchoice.org/map.asp).

The 2011 Montana Legislature promised us it would concentrate on economic issues, but then embarrassed our state nationally with its crazy cultural agenda. I found myself apologizing to my friends across the country on Facebook. The extremists who support big government when it comes to personal matters spent more time fighting women's rights, medical marijuana, and equal rights in Missoula than they did creating jobs for Montanans.

In Montana, the state GOP platform says that homosexuality should be illegal. In this, as with other cultural matters, the party is out of touch and behind the times. Almost one-third of Republicans supported legalizing same-sex marriage in a 2011 Gallup poll. More importantly, our future leaders are way ahead of their bed-snooping elders. Over 70 percent of 18- to 34-year-olds support legalizing same-sex marriage. This is up 16 percentage points from 2010.

I can remember when the Republican Party was a different party. In 1980, I was a delegate to the GOP Colorado convention and we were so proud that we were successful in keeping anti-choice zealots off the floor, knowing they would divide and destroy the party. The question for the state of Montana in 2012 is how much cultural distractions and the debacle of the 2011 legislative session decide this election?

Blocking action

The party has painted itself into a corner on cultural issues. Ideologues have closed the door and hung out "Not Welcome" signs blocking centrist or center-right candidates who can't pass narrow litmus tests on cultural issues.

Even if such candidates could pass through the ideologues' fine-filter mesh, could they win a general election, given the current cultural war that the Republicans have positioned themselves to lose? Do Americans want a Republican controlled Senate in Washington, D.C., to mimic the extremism and dysfunction of the Republican controlled House? How will this dynamic affect the Rehberg vs. Tester Senate race?

How many Montanans realize they were duped when 2010 Republicans with a strong economic message turned into 2011 Republicans stirring up fear and polarization? Will this finally be the end of the crazy Republicans and the return of the thinking Republicans? We can only hope.

A.J. Otjen of Laurel teaches business courses at Montana State University Billings. She is Montana coordinator for Republicans for Environmental Protection.

Response printed on April 24, 2012

By golly, was I heartened to read A.J. Otjen April 14 opinion, "Will 2012 see return of thinking GOP?" about actual thinking GOP. Do any of us suppose this will actually happen?

If so, I certainly look forward to seeing and meeting them. I am hoping that A.J. would consider running again as it would be such a refreshing change to what we experienced in the last Legislature and what seems to be happening on the nation's front as I speak. Maybe she is starting a trend. Let us all hope so.

2011

*M*issoulian

GOP should support less government

November 28, 2011 Guest column by A.J. OTJEN

There are currently nine candidates running for governor in the Republican primary, but will any one of them face the tough issue that the Montana Supreme Court is considering now? On Aug. 4, Montana Supreme Court heard an appeal giving same-sex couples the protections that heterosexual couples enjoy. We should demand that our Republican leaders support this decision. But, the Montana Republican party platform says homosexual acts should remain illegal.

Apparently, the party that favors smaller, less intrusive government wants bigger, more intrusive government when it comes to our domestic arrangements. Three's a crowd in the bedroom, folks.

Worse, the party line doesn't fit with what most Republicans think. The latest Gallup poll says that 85 percent of Republicans want their candidates to focus on the economy, not social issues.

It will be increasingly difficult for Republicans to win general elections if party leaders try to block the Supreme Court ruling or this troubling clause stays in the Republican state platform. Almost two-thirds of independents supported legalizing same-sex marriage in a 2010 Gallup poll.

Anecdotal evidence from online posts shows thousands of voters saying they would vote Republican except for the GOP's rigid stance on gay issues.

Almost one-third of Republicans supported legalizing same-sex marriage in the 2010 Gallup poll. Over 70 percent of 18- to 34-year-olds support legalizing same-sex marriage, up 16 percentage points from 2010. This "overwhelming" number in favor of marriage equality "makes the trend toward growing acceptance both clear and unstoppable," says Jon Walker at Firedoglake.

Six states allow legal same-sex marriages: New York, Connecticut, Iowa, Massachusetts, New Hampshire and Vermont. The District of Columbia also allows them. While five of those states are considered "blue," their legalizing of same-sex marriages are a sign that times are changing.

As Gallup's Frank Newport said: "At the moment, those advocating changes in constitutions and laws to allow same-sex marriage in additional states can take heart in the apparent shift in national sentiment in their direction."

This shift means Montana Republicans are resisting a groundswell. Soon enough, equal rights for gays will trump states' rights.

The repeal of "Don't Ask, Don't Tell" for our armed forces was a victory for individual freedom. Barry Goldwater, who once said, "I don't care if they are straight, I only care if they shoot straight," would be proud.

As usual, Goldwater was ahead of his time. More than 72 percent supported repealing "Don't Ask, Don't Tell" according to a November 2010 CNN poll, up from 67 percent in September.

Majorities of weekly churchgoers (60 percent) and conservatives (58 percent) also support repealing the policy (Gallup, 2009).

Repealing "Don't Ask, Don't Tell" also was a victory for fiscal responsibility. A 2003 Government Accountability Office study identified almost $200 million in costs for the first 10 years of "Don't Ask, Don't Tell." A follow-up study by an expert commission put these costs at more than $363 million.

Over the long term, Republican candidates cannot expect their opposition to equal rights for gays to help them. If support for gay marriage continues accelerating as fast as it has in the past two years, supporters will outnumber opponents roughly 56-40 in the general population by November 2012.

Another straw in the wind: The Log Cabin Republicans and GOProud have been invited to the Conservative Political Action Conference for the last few years. The facts are clear. Republicans all over the country and here in Montana support gay families. Delegates will have the opportunity to change the Republican state party platform. We should lead and not follow on this issue.

The State Supreme Court is expected to make a ruling by the end of 2012. If we Republicans let this platform clause stay in place again in 2012, we will once again experience millions of Montana Republican homophobia news stories living forever online. We will lose forever voters who would be Republicans but for our stubborn resistance to gay rights. We will lose the big offices in the state. And we will be wrong.

A.J. Otjen is a professor at Montana State University-Billings, and was a GOP candidate for Congress in 2010.

14

Response:

From Eternity To Here

~the voice of injustice is silence

After My Own Heart

Nov **29** by D Gregory Smith

A.J. Otjen, University of Montana Professor and 2010 GOP Congressional Candidate has an Op-Ed in the Missoulian that flies in the face of the arguments by Treasure State Politics about <u>LGBT rights</u> (see previous post) and takes on the Montana GOP's Notorious Platform Plank:

I am delighted and cautiously optimistic.

Of course I want her to be a bellwether, and having A.J. Otjen singing "The Times, They Are A-Changing" (with statistics) might be the wake-up call the Montana GOP needs. But will they hear it?

The Tea-Party Christianists seem to have a loud voice, if not large numbers- and the fact that this plank was "sneaked in" past the majority of delegates- as some maintain- doesn't leave me with a helluva lot of faith in the process.

I want to believe it. I do. I like what she's singin', God bless her. It's rational, reasonable, and backed by scientific data.

But I know a few people who'll run to unplug the speakers as fast as they can. Especially because it's rational, reasonable and backed by scientific data.

Sigh.

15

BILLINGS GAZETTE

Guest opinion: Land conservation shouldn't be partisan debate

October 08, 2011 By A.J. OTJEN

"Conservation rollback legislation stirs up rather than calms down the excessive tension and polarization we see in conservation debates."

Descendants of William Clark recently gave to the Chinook Tribe a replacement for the ocean-going canoe that Lewis and Clark took during a dark moment on their Voyage of Discovery.

The gift ceremony was a heartwarming event that connected people across cultures and generations across time. More than two centuries after their travels, Lewis and Clark's journey continues to inspire us.

There is no better place for Americans to experience all that Lewis and Clark experienced than the Upper Missouri River Breaks National Monument, a treasure chest of Montana history and heritage.

Unfortunately, Rep. Dennis Rehberg keeps rejecting the idea of the monument's establishment a decade ago, backs legislation to weaken the law that made the Breaks monument possible, and supports another bill to end protection for backcountry treasures.

Rehberg has introduced the Montana Land Sovereignty Act, which was aired at a recent House subcommittee hearing.

His bill would water down the Antiquities Act, a law that authorizes presidents to establish national monuments on public lands that have outstanding natural and historic features that are worthy of protection.

In addition, he is co-sponsoring the Wilderness and Roadless Areas Release Act, which would end protection for at least 43 million acres of road less public lands across the West, including more than 5 million acres of wild forests and prairies in Montana.

They include diamonds in the rough like Frenchman's Creek in Phillips County. Frenchman's Creek is a strange warren of badlands and coulees where, Field & Stream blogger Hal Herring recently wrote, wily old bucks have found a refuge from roads and noise, offering a sportsman willing to hike through tough country some of the best hunting anywhere in America.

Conservation rollback legislation stirs up rather than calms down the excessive tension and polarization we see in conservation debates.

For example, the fog of angry rhetoric around the Antiquities Act obscures an important fact. The narrowly tailored law can only be invoked to protect special lands already within the federal domain. It does not apply to state-owned lands or private property.

Fifteen presidents from both parties, most recently George W. Bush, have used the Antiquities Act to establish national monuments protecting treasures as breathtaking as the Grand Canyon and as historically important as Thomas Edison's laboratory.

President William Howard Taft, for example, used the Antiquities Act in 1910 to protect what is now the Big Hole National Battlefield in southwestern Montana, which honors combatants who fought and died in the Nez Perce War of 1877.

Historic preservation and conserving lands of outstanding natural beauty should not be matters that stir the flames of angry partisanship.

We know Rehberg could lead us away from such unproductive rhetoric. We know because Rehberg has shown that he understands the broad appeal and long-term benefit of conservation. He played an important role in securing federal funds to protect the Meeteetse Spires, a striking geologic formation in Carbon County.

When the Clark family and the Chinooks worked together to right an old wrong, they set a great example for the rest of us. We ask Rehberg to follow that example, put aside polarizing legislation, and help Montanans find common ground on conservation.

A.J. Otjen of Laurel is the Montana coordinator for Republicans for Environmental Protection. She was an unsuccessful 2008 GOP candidate for the House seat held by Denny Rehberg.

Guest opinion: America needs laws that protect clean air, water

August 15, 2011 By A.J. OTJEN and JIM DIPESO

"Fiscal and environmental stewardship are two sides of the same coin."

No matter how carefully energy companies go about their business, accidents like the Yellowstone River oil spill are inevitable.

Exxon actually has a good record for tracking their performance. We know this because there is a cop on the beat to make sure pollution control standards are set and enforced. It's part of the social contract for maintaining a livable environment for everyone.

That was the thinking that went into the passage of laws like the Clean Air Act and Clean Water Act by bipartisan majorities a generation ago. Congress gave the job of enforcing those laws to the Environmental Protection Agency, established by President Richard Nixon in 1970.

It's hard to understand the thinking behind efforts to weaken those laws — such as the appropriations bill pending in the House that is littered with "riders" that would throttle enforcement of anti-pollution laws. We don't want to leave our children a huge debt but we also don't want to leave them a dirty planet to inherit. Fiscal and environmental stewardship are two sides of the same coin.

Other provisions in the bill would impose disproportionate budget cuts on conservation and clean-water programs.

And the bill would do little to correct America's fiscal imbalances. Indeed, if EPA were put out of business entirely, the budget savings would be equivalent to a mere two-tenths of 1 percent of the federal budget.

Here is what it would do in its present form:

Enact budget language that in effect would block limits on emissions of airborne toxins from cement kilns.

Likewise, block cleanup of mercury emissions from coal-fired power plants.

Chop a revolving loan fund for sewage treatment plant construction by more than half.

Cut a voluntary endangered-wildlife conservation program by 95 percent.

Reduce the Land and Water Conservation Fund 80 percent below last year's level and 95 percent below the fully authorized amount of $900 million per year. These drastic cuts would affect Montana directly. The state has received $36 million for open space and recreation projects in all 56 counties. The fund has supported conservation of great Montana treasures, including the Meeteetse Spires on the eastern slope of the Beartooth Mountains, and conservation easements on the Rocky Mountain Front.

There are more such provisions. No one should argue that conservation and pollution control programs should be exempt from budget scrutiny. Taxpayers deserve assurances that they're getting the most value out of every dollar spent on keeping air and water clean and on protecting America's backcountry and wildlife heritage.

The appropriations bill under consideration, however, goes well beyond careful scrutiny. It has the appearance, instead, of a spasmodic attack, rooted in an unfortunate and inaccurate perception that protecting the environment is strictly for "liberals."

That perception might be politically correct in Republican circles, but it doesn't fit at all with the traditional conservative ethic of stewardship. Russell Kirk, the conservative thinker who was Ronald Reagan's favorite author, once said, "Nothing is more conservative than conservation."

Kirk's ideas are rooted in the thinking of Edmund Burke, the statesman widely regarded as the founder of modern conservatism. Burke taught that society is an intergenerational contract, which imposes a duty on today's generation to protect what it has inherited on behalf of generations to come.

That's what stewardship is all about — taking care of what we have so we can pass on something good to our kids. That goes for the nation's finances and it goes for the air, water, and natural resources that underpin our civilization.

Lawmakers who call themselves conservatives (and the corporations that support them) would do well to ponder those conservative values — before they weaken common-sense laws that could prevent the next Yellowstone River spill.

Jim DiPeso of Seattle is policy director of Republicans for Environmental Protection (REP America), and A.J. Otjen of Laurel is the state coordinator.

Guest opinion: Let's agree to reduce waste in the U.S.

June 25, 2011 By A.J. OTJEN

"Three hundred million of us are setting a standard of consumption that is about to be emulated by over 3 billion Chinese and Indians."

We don't have to agree on climate change.

But we do have to agree on behavior change when it comes to consumption. There are nearly 7 billion people on the planet (projected to be 9 billion by 2050) and we 300 million Americans are 5 percent of the world's population. But we consume 25 percent of the world's resources. Imagine if everyone in the world consumed at the rate we Americans do.

Three hundred million of us are setting a standard of consumption that is about to be emulated by over 3 billion Chinese and Indians. Our standard of living is spreading throughout the world.

Each American consumes an average 150 gallons of water every day, a per capita rate which is almost four times as much as Asia and twice as much as Europe. It is almost 10 times as much as Africa, according to Mindfully.org (www.mindfully.org/Sustainability/Americans-Consume-24percent.htm).

Almost 80 percent of diseases in so called "developing" countries are associated with water, causing some three million early deaths. For example, 5,000 children die every day from diarrhea, or one every 17 seconds, according to Worldometers (www.worldometers.info/water/).

Over 70 percent of the world's water supply goes towards producing food, which must increase as the population increases. China and India, where water demand is rising the most, are considered two of the most at-risk countries for running short of clean water.

The world currently produces enough food to supply 2,700 calories per person per day. Although that could feed the world, distribution bottlenecks, such as lack of adequate roads and cold storage, results in waste that causes millions to go hungry.

Americans eat 200 billion more calories per day than necessary — enough to feed 80 million people. While millions of people around the world face malnutrition, one-third of the U.S. population is significantly overweight. Americans spend $30 billion annually on diet programs.

We produce huge quantities of solid waste, an average of 4.5 pounds per person each day. Americans go through 2,000 plastic bottles every five minutes, 60,000 plastic bags every five

20

seconds, and discard 426,000 cell phones a day. The average American office worker goes through around 500 disposable cups every year. Americans throw away 570 diapers per second. That's 49 million diapers per day.

Not all the trash is properly disposed of. Right now there is a trash patch in the Pacific Ocean spanning an area twice the size of Texas, according to How stuff works(http://science.howstuffworks.com/environmental/earth/oceanography/great-pacific-garbage-patch.htm).

Industrial economies run on huge quantities of cheap, portable energy. There are over 10 trillion barrels of oil (4 trillion of "easy" oil) identified as available on the planet or less than 100 years left at the current rate of consumption of about 90 million barrels a day. We consume almost 20 million barrels a day. Multiply that by 10 and the world will consume 200 million barrels a day. Whether that quantity can be found in the earth for the next few generations is an open question. The estimate for peak production of conventional oil is less than 40 years, according to the Post Carbon Institute (www.energybulletin.net/node/4929).

We don't have to agree on climate change but we can agree on simple, responsible changes that reduce waste and unnecessary consumption. Use real silverware and cups. Don't waste. Eat healthy. Turn out the lights. Pick up after ourselves. Remember the frugal wisdom of our grandparents.

A.J. Otjen of Laurel teaches business courses at Montana State University Billings and is state coordinator for Republicans for Environmental Protection.

Response printed July 02, 2011

Regarding the June 25 op-ed piece by A.J. Otjen ("Let's agree to reduce waste in the U.S."), I congratulate the author on two things.

First, she's right: Americans have been wasteful ever since we colonized the wealthiest (and last) frontier in the New World. We thought nothing about using up the incredible abundant resources, leaving a depleted landscape and moving west to start doing the same thing all over again. We as a nation have never come to grips with the kind of lifelong grinding poverty and limitations in which many other countries live constantly — poverty which breeds an unhealthy competition for scarcer and scarcer resources.

Second, she's right, too, in urging us as Americans to agree on something — and doing what we can on a personal or organizational basis to use (and waste) less. Every social issue becomes politicized, with each side bent on beating the other over the head politically.

I'm glad to see the Republicans have somebody who's civilly trying to bring our attention to things that urgently need doing.

BILLINGS GAZETTE

Guest opinion: What Obama and Ryan don't say in their budget plans

April 30, 2011 By A.J. Otjen

The United States has a revenue problem as much as a spending problem. Using the trends of the last 100 years, by 2030 we will have a GDP of over $23 trillion per year. Using current budget percentage rates we will have a federal budget of almost $6 trillion if we stay at 25 percent of GDP, which seems reasonable for a first-class country. But we only take in 18 percent in revenues. This is why we keep going more and more in debt.

To pay off our current debt of $14 trillion in 20 years, we need part of our budget to be surplus now. Let's assume that 20 percent of the debt will never be paid off, as it is owed to ourselves in the form of pensions, mutual funds and personal retirement funds that will continue to roll over through generations. Thus, to pay off $12 trillion in 20 years we need a surplus of $600 billion a year, simplistically, paid to the debt.

Using the same trend analysis, in 20 years we will have another 60 million in our U.S. population and they will be almost twice as productive, from $47,000 per capita today, to $72,000 per capita in 2030. So it is likely that the tax base along with the economy will grow to cover the revenues/budget we need if we also do the following:

Put $600 billion a year of the current spending level toward the debt.

Cut $100 billion from the military budget, and then keep it at no more than 20 percent of the federal budget overall.

Cut billions out of the $400 billion spent on interest payments. Forty percent of the debt is owed to the Federal Reserve. For every 1 percent change in interest rate we pay per year, we pay about $100 billion and we currently average over 3 percent, so negotiate this down in order to spend less on interest payments. And as we have less debt, our Treasury bill will go down as well.

Cut oil subsidies by $50 billion, out of the $75 billion we spend now.

Cut billions out of the $500 billion we spend on health care entitlements — not with fewer services but with lower costs. We will lower costs of health care with competition for basic care via high deductibles and thus reform the health care system itself, and have regional health care funds for catastrophic needs, to take the burden off of business.

Move eligibility for Medicare and Social Security for everyone under 40 to age 70. After all, 70 is the new 60.

Invest $200 billion in infrastructure every year. Go into long-term debt for long-term investment and take advantage of lower interest rates. That is only 20 percent of what is actually needed.

Increase revenues to 25 percent of GDP with the higher burden on those who have been able to take the most advantage of the great infrastructure of this great country.

We must all come to some common understandings of where we want to be as a country in 20 years. This discussion is not about the little domestic spending items that bog us down. It is about the big things. We are a great nation and it takes money to make it run. We can debate how revenues are raised as long as it is fair, as long as it gives incentives to for a healthy middle class and builds jobs here at home. And as long as it keeps us a clean, healthy and free land of prosperity for all.

A.J. Otjen of Laurel is a professor of marketing at Montana State University Billings. She was an unsuccessful candidate in the 2010 Republican primary for Montana's U.S. House seat.

2010

Guest opinion: GOP teachers push agenda to support public schools

August 14, 2010 By A.J. OTJEN

Republican members of the Montana Education Association traveled to Washington, D.C., last month to give input to Dennis Rehberg, Jon Tester and Max Baucus for the reauthorization of the Elementary and Secondary Education Act, for a while known as No Child Left Behind.

We first wanted to revamp the accountability system and restore balance between federal, state and locals in education. The new policies have to be more locally driven and have accountability by the due process of tenure as well as new ideas based on growth with educator input. We also pushed the concept of rural wireless broadband technology to support local small schools in small towns.

Karen Lewis of Helena, Kathy Kuntz of Great Falls and I joined fellow Republican educators from 40 states at a gathering of NEA Republican Leaders at the National Education Association in Washington, D.C., to strategize about ways to improve public education by electing and influencing leaders who will speak up for education and kids.

The Montana Education Association sponsored a booth at the Republican Platform Convention. One item on the Republican Party platform states that the Republican Party is for tax credits for attending alternative education to public schools. The Montana Constitution clearly states that the legislation shall not make any indirect appropriations or payment from any public fund or monies for any sectarian purpose or to aid any church, school, academy, etc. For the Republican Party to suggest that a tax credit is not a reduction in revenues for public schools or an indirect appropriation from a public fund or money is dishonest. This should be removed from the platform, as Republicans have always been supporters of our constitution.

Another item of our education platform is for flexible accreditation, which ultimately has the goal of right to work with less pay for teachers, or the right to hire teachers who don't have official accreditation. We all want to lower costs, but we can do that with the virtual academy, which will keep standards high and costs low while keeping schools open in the smaller communities. Education is about 35 percent of the economy in small towns, so that cutting

24

schools and flexible accreditation is not the solution for cutting costs. Technology is the answer for keeping them viable and accredited.

Republican educators make up nearly one-third of the 3.2 million-member NEA and about 30 percent of the MEA-MFT. Republican educators are like most workers who want to work with great colleagues and do not want to see nonperforming workers continue to be rewarded or employed or paid ever increasing salaries. We support tenure or due process to dismiss these employees. Much of our discussion in Washington was to try to understand why so much of the public discussion about education included teacher bashing and a misunderstanding with tenure. Educators across the country are working to reform education.

Nationwide, we spend 7 percent of gross domestic product (about $1 trillion including all levels of government with about 10 percent controlled at the federal level). Montana's population is about 0.3 percent of the nation, which means we should spend about $3 billion when we spend just over $2 billion. Either we are spending too little or the nation is spending too much. But why are we bashing teachers as the culprits?

If unions are demanding that administrators follow due process and do their jobs in order to dismiss a teacher, good. Teachers do everything they can for the benefit of students. It is only right that that the teachers union does everything it can for the benefit of teachers and therefore education.

A.J. Otjen of Laurel has worked in the private sector and taught business at the university level. She was an unsuccessful GOP candidate for U.S. House this year. For more information about NEA's principles for the reauthorization of ESEA, visit www.nea.org/home/1335.htm.

4&20 blackbirds

Blogging the politics and culture of Missoula and Montana and everywhere else beyond.

June 3, 2010

by jhwygirl

I ruminated in a comment or two around here on how Rehberg really failed to engage in the primary. I had heard nothing of any forums – while I know that county Democratic organizations around the state held forums for their congressional candidates. It's hard for any candidate that doesn't really get the opportunity to engage, side-by-side, with their competitors. But hey – that's Rehberg arrogance. Besides that, I know that Pogo Possum expressed an interest in hearing more from A.J. Otjen….so here you are folks. Information is power.

From A.J. Otjen:

In January, Denny promised me that we would have a Republican Primary Debate. It is now less than a week before the election and his schedule as never let that happen. It is just never in the best interest of the incumbent to debate. I have met him in public and have asked him specific questions and every time he says…"we are not going to debate now". So when? Tell us why you are now fighting for a balanced budget without getting specific about spending cuts and where to find revenues. Tell us why you have sponsored hundreds of bills and sent out thousands of press releases that go absolutely nowhere. Tell us why you vote against a stimulus package and then beg for the money to fund projects in Montana.

I am on the road doing my last tour of Montana before the election and do meet Mark French in public forums. He does have a following like a preacher has sheep. After one of his tirades, one of his followers even said as I stood up…"good luck following that". Throughout these events, it is always clear that he has no handle on facts. He is all fire. (The conservative conference in Missoula helped him raise money in one day) I call him the dramatic candidate and myself the practical candidate, undaunted by his brimstone. I am undaunted by his misrepresentation of me saying 'Ms. Otjen who hates the constitution.' I say, for that..you have to call me Dr. Otjen. Almost every male in my family has been in combat defending the constitution.

I have enjoyed most of all going into the French and Rehberg areas and turning folks around. It works mainly with small groups. When people have time to listen. When people do not get caught up with emotion and loyalties, the facts always win. There is so much hope for where we can go with politics if we treat it like an elephant that we eat one bite at a time. Even the TEA party. If they were truly just about Taxes Enough Already, maybe they would be OK. When we hold them to that….they calm down. I asked them if they were about anything else…and they refused to say. I confronted them with their misrepresentation of me..and a few have been embarrassed. I confronted the College Republicans with their own embarrassing but humorous recruitment video and called them Fox Mimics who needed different students in their ranks.

But we could have one tremendous bite right now with this election. We could change so much about Montana politics with the GOP primary turning out reasonable Republicans going forward to the general. It is states with open primaries like ours that will lead the nation back to having two equal and reasonable parties. Instead we have one in power at a time, which always leads to absolute power corrupting absolutely. Extremists on either side cannot keep controlling our agendas. The issues facing us right now will change the way we live just 30 years from now. Knowing that, and seeing how the future could be devastating or fantastic, is why I decided to run.

Comments:

She got my vote in the primary. There will be a lot of crossover voting in Gallatin County. The Tea Party and Constitutionalist Party crossovers will vote for French. The Democrat crossovers will vote for AJ.

Wow...wish AJ had talked like this a little sooner. Already filled out my ballot, democratic, but I really liked what I just heard from her here. Thanks for sharing jhwygirl.

What a pitiful congressman Denny Rehberg is. He won't even discuss ideas with the far, far right (French) and the moderate Republican (Otjen). He's ignoring the voters. What arrogance.

A.J. did a nice TV spot. Saying "the Republican Party is off course" takes some chutzpa.

However, for this race, I have to point out that the 4 key components in a successful political campaign consist of Message, Organization, Money and Management. Though you have provided your message, you have been unsuccessful with the other three components. Your future success will depend on mastering all four of these key campaign elements. Though

If I thought it would help, I'd cross over and vote for Otjen. But really, I think the Democratic primary is so important; not just the congressional race but the down ticket races, too.

"Besides that, I know that Pogo Possum expressed an interest in hearing more from A.J. Otjen..."

These women are challenging the establishment — never an easy task.

Note to A. J. Otjen – Always glad to see new upcoming candidates take the stage especially women candidates with new points of view. You have a future in Montana politics down the road. I wish you well in future races.

The MONTANA STANDARD
mtstandard.com

Candidate statements — U.S. House seat -- A.J. Otjen, Republican

May 28, 2010 By A.J. Otjen

(Editor's note: The Standard invited the eight candidates vying for Montana's lone seat in the U.S. House of Representatives to submit guest opinions of up to 750 words. One will be published each weekday through June 4.)

For me, the Republican Party stands for economic discipline first and foremost. I want to balance the budget, something this Congress has not done for the last decade. We cannot keep adding to the debt with operating costs. Our jobless economy is stuck as long as we cannot manage our country's business better than we do.

I have identified $900 billion in cuts to the budget, but that leaves $600 billion in revenues that we still need. There is no way we can cut income taxes now down from the 10 to 35 percent rates that exist today, practically the lowest in the history of federal income taxes. In 1980 the debt was $1 trillion. Reagan reduced the top income tax rate from 80 percent to 50 percent and kept it there for most of his term. He took it finally to 39 percent. He also increased military spending more than it had ever been since WW II. This was in all practicality a stimulus package doing the most to stimulate the economy at the time.

We have the last 30 years of results of tax cuts and how they affect our economy. The federal revenues we need to balance the annual budget have never caught up as a result of these tax reductions, even if we had maintained normal spending. The fact that we have increased spending has resulted in even worse deficits. Today we have a $14 trillion debt and a 35 percent top tax rate. We will never balance the budget if we cut taxes now.

However, I have a published a tax reform plan for small businesses that would stimulate the economy by letting them keep their cash in retained earnings, prior to paying income tax on profit. Small businesses do create jobs and investment. This would also keep cash in the banks, putting liquidity in the marketplace which would have prevented the need for TARP.

For all issues involving health care, the environment, etc., as much as possible I believe in economic incentives more than legislation so that our businesses will spend their money on scientists and engineers instead of lawyers and lobbyists.

29

It is time for us to focus on the most important issues for the future of our country. These are our economy, how we manage and protect our resources and how we treat each other. I have a technology background and I understand how we can bridge the gap between energy and the environment so that we are the best in the world at harnessing our resources. That's why the National Republicans for Environmental Protections have endorsed me in this election.

For health care, we need to take the bill that has already passed and make it work. Without reform, we will never balance the budget and a great percentage of our economy will be based on health care.

I support market-based reforms in health care to lower costs. I also support stiffer penalties for fraud and frivolous lawsuits. We have got to get more technology and transparency in administrative areas. But primarily, we need economic incentives, both private and public, to have healthier lifestyles. Over 75 percent of the costs are in chronic disease caused by the way we take care of ourselves and the foods we eat. This comprehensive reform is where the care bill must go from here and Republicans can and must lead the way on this issue.

When some in our Republican Party say we stand for faith and family that implies that the Democrats do not love their families or have faith, when they do. Everyone has the right to believe what they want about complex social issues. The point is the government does not. It is time for us to stand up and say it loud. The social issues have divided our country and we need to go back to the time when we were focused on the economic and resource and world issues important to our future.

Too often these days we have become bullies on both sides and it has got to stop. We need two reasonable parties if we have any hope of hearing each other without fear. I look to the Democratic Party to clean up its own team. And the failed, fall-in-line Republican Congress of the last decade is not the Congress we should return to Washington. It is time to elect new Republicans to go to Washington and get this party and country working again.

Comments:

No republican can get Republican Party support unless they adhere to the specific republican platform. Trust me, it is the same for the democrats.

I know personally because I was instructed by the Ventura County Republican Committee chairman.

In other words, acceptable republican-backed candidates means more of the same old corruption, broken promises and usurpation of our rights.

Amen A.J.! Reality, not slogans or slander. I like this a lot. You seem like a person that those of us that are sick and tired of the same old party lines can get behind. You remind me of the old Republican Party I used to be a member of before it went in the ditch. Out of all the House candidates statements, I like your's best.

Sensible, reasoned, practical. That certainly puts her at odds with politics as usual. Hers is a conservatism that should ring true to Montana voters.

The curious case of AJ Otjen

by: Jay Stevens
Wed Apr 28, 2010 at 07:41:49 AM MST

The *Billings Gazette* has been running profiles of the Republican candidates for Montana's US House seat. The latest was of A.J. Otjen:

Otjen is a Republican who doesn't talk about tax cuts. In fact, she said tax cuts don't work to jump-start the economy and increase revenues in the long term.

"We've got the data that proves that," she said.

She doesn't talk about abortion, except to say she doesn't think it should be illegal. She thinks the words like "faith and family" that many Republicans use to describe themselves ignore the fact that Democrats love their families, too, and they go to church.

She is running to give voice to those traditional Republicans who do not define themselves by wedge social issues, which might rally the party base but, she says, do little to take on the nation's larger problems.

"I would like to go back to the days when social issues did not dominate the Republican Party," she said.

Likewise on Otjen's website (subtitled, "A Teddy Roosevelt Republican"), her issues page demonstrates how she's different than your typical contemporary Montana Republican: Pro-education. An opponent of "the War on Terror." A fierce advocate of privacy, from the bedroom to boardroom. Against across-the-board tax cuts. A supporter of a Green Economy, but through tax credits and incentives. She supports a tax on high fructose corn syrup. And so on.

A Republican friend noted on Facebook the other day that "Otjen diverges from the GOP on more than social issues - she's for higher taxes, she voted for Obama (and is still a supporter) and supports the recent healthcare bill that passed."

But that's ignoring Otjen's real conservative values. She's a true deficit hawk - you can't erase a deficit by cutting taxes. She favors market solutions to problems - tax incentives and credits to businesses who embrace green tech and reduce carbon, as opposed to a carbon tax. On social issues, it's more accurate to classify her as libertarian than liberal. And supporting the recent health care bill hardly makes you a liberal - the bill, after all, was pretty much written by the Heritage Foundation. Open the insurance market to competition and provide subsidies to those that can't afford premiums. Even the individual mandate is a conservative invention. And if you've been reading this blog and its comments for any length of time, you'll know that supporting Obama doesn't necessarily tarnish your conservative credentials.

In short, Otjen's is what a Republican would look like if a Republican laid aside partisanship and applied pragmatic, conservative values to the very real problems afflicting the nation. The opposite of, say, Dennis Rehberg, who's achieved next to nothing in Congress other than riding along on the wave of GOP support for the worst excesses of the Bush administration: deficit, economic collapse, war, torture.

Otjen is a moderate. And if you think there really is such a thing as the "radical center" just waiting to burst out and shuck off the manacles of party politics, then she should be the leading candidate in this race. But that she's an afterthought in this race, no more highly regarded than, say, Mark French (who wants the US government to run on "Biblical principles" as defined by Mark French), tells us a lot about the current state of Republican politics, which not only lacks for real solutions to global warming, joblessness, and the health care crisis, but fails to even acknowledge those problems exist.

The Republican party has devolved from a political party with policy goals to a group of people clinging onto echo-chamber sound bites, like Titanic survivors to a life raft. And Otjen, who doesn't kowtow to the rhetoric, will be tossed off into the sea.

Comments:

Moderate? Hardly. Otjen leans more liberal, which is only slightly more center than progressive.

Her campaign has little to do with the Republican platform, and more to do with trying to direct the GOP towards her little, one person life raft.

She will be an extinct RINO on June 9th - fortunately.

BILLINGS GAZETTE

Rehberg challenger Otjen diverges from party on traditional social issues

April 26, 2010 By JENNIFER McKEE

HELENA — Republican congressional candidate A.J. Otjen has known real success in life, but the thing that gives her the most pleasure is simple and sweet:

"I think I made my mother proud," she said in a recent telephone interview from her log home outside Laurel.

Otjen, 52, is one of three Republicans whose names will appear on the June 8 primary ballot, which also includes Mark French and five-time incumbent Rep. Denny Rehberg. Otjen is a political newcomer and a bit of an oddity on Montana's political landscape.

She is a single, self-made woman — an out-of-stater who moved here in 2003 after retiring in her 40s as a marketing vice president for the Sprint telecommunications company in Kansas City.

But it's not the fact that she is a woman in what is mostly a man's game or an Oklahoma native in an arena where "Montana roots" are real currency that makes Otjen so unusual.

It's what she says.

Otjen is a Republican who doesn't talk about tax cuts. In fact, she said tax cuts don't work to jump-start the economy and increase revenues in the long term.

"We've got the data that proves that," she said.

She doesn't talk about abortion, except to say she doesn't think it should be illegal. She thinks the words like "faith and family" that many Republicans use to describe themselves ignore the fact that Democrats love their families, too, and they go to church.

She is running to give voice to those traditional Republicans who do not define themselves by wedge social issues, which might rally the party base but, she says, do little to take on the nation's larger problems.

"I would like to go back to the days when social issues did not dominate the Republican Party," she said.

34

Those traditional Republican values run deep in Otjen's family.

Her grandfather was one of the first Republicans to run for governor of Oklahoma in 1942, in the days when Oklahoma's politics were dominated by Democrats. What's amazing, Otjen said, is how close he came to winning.

"He lost by a couple thousand votes," she said. "He was quite the guy."

The youngest of three children, Otjen was raised by her father, an attorney, and her mother, "a very competent housewife" who believed well-brought up young ladies should know how to ride a horse and shoot a gun, Otjen said.

"I do both of those well," she said.

Otjen's parents divorced when she was 15, and she said her growing up was "like any typical, challenging childhood."

Otjen earned a bachelor's degree in marketing from the University of Missouri and jumped into her professional life, landing on her feet in Denver. And she believes in creating real incentives to bring down costs of things such as health care. Otjen said she would support a tax on fatty foods, using that money to build bike paths or to have more recess in public schools.

"I like economic incentives more than legislation," she said.

Otjen was also working toward her master's degree in business administration at night at the University of Colorado in Boulder, which she attained in 1984.

For a while, she ran her own marketing company in Denver. She got married and eventually moved to Boulder City, Nev., where she got a job as the director of marketing for telecommunications giant Sprint Corp.

She and her husband also owned the Grand Canyon Airlines, which did fly-over flights of the nearby Grand Canyon.

Later, Otjen moved to Kansas City, Mo., where she worked as a vice president of marketing for Sprint's emerging wireless business. She retired from Sprint in 2001. Two years later, she moved to Montana to take a job teaching marketing at Montana State University Billings.

In 1999, she and her husband divorced. They had no children.

Otjen may not always talk like a latter-day Republican, but when she starts talking budgets, her party's roots sound through. While she doesn't believe in cutting taxes in a time of record deficits, she can run through a list of billions of dollars in cuts from almost every federal agency.

Missoula *Independent*

Up to the challenge

Otjen pushes Rehberg in promising primary

April 15, 2010 by <u>George Ochenski</u>

It's been a long time since Montana's lone congressman, Republican Denny Rehberg, had an interesting contender for his seat in the U.S. House of Representatives. This year, however, is different. There are four Democrats vying in the primary to oppose Rehberg in the general election, and we'll take a look at those in a future column. But one of the most intriguing aspects of this year's election is Rehberg's primary opponent, Dr. A.J. Otjen, of Laurel. A talented and attractive woman, she just might give Rehberg a run in the highest-profile race of this year's mid-term elections.

Otjen is currently a tenured professor of Integrated Marketing Communications at Montana State University-Billings and, if the awards won by her students are any indication, she's a very capable mentor. Besides holding a doctorate in economics, Otjen brings real world experience to her task, having retired in her 40s from her position as vice president of the telecommunications giant, Sprint Corporation. As she told Lee's Capitol Bureau Chief, Chuck Johnson, this week: "The difference between me and Denny is I have actually experienced balancing billion-dollar budgets, and he's been part of the Congress that has failed to do it the past 10 years."

Of course having Republicans tout their fiscal conservatism is nothing new—they all do. The record, however, is quite different than the campaign pledges. From Ronald Reagan right up through George W. Bush, Republican presidents and Republican-dominated congresses have consistently spent the nation deep into debt. The two main issues driving Republican-caused debt have been onerous and expensive wars and the party's foundational belief in tax cuts for the wealthy, of which George W. Bush excelled at both.

On the tax issue Otjen's pretty straight up—and not what you'd expect. As she said this week: "When you're talking about balancing the budget, you can't cut income taxes. Right now, income taxes are 10 percent to 35 percent, practically the lowest in the history of the income tax. You can't cut taxes now."

Coming from a Republican, that's quite a statement. Unfortunately, it's also one with which many of the party faithful are likely to disagree vehemently. According to basic Republican economic tenets, the primary way to stimulate the economy and spur investment is through cutting taxes. The main recipients of this largesse, whether they actually invest anything in the economy or not, have traditionally been the largest corporations and the wealthiest individuals in the nation. Then of course there's the Tea Party, which could affect the Republican primary, and the "Tea" stands for "taxed enough already." Win or lose, however, it seems likely we'll be seeing more of the interesting Dr. Otjen in our political future.

On war spending Otjen hasn't offered much in the way of specifics so far—nor have most other candidates or sitting politicos. Her website, however, puts forth what might be seen as conflicting views. While saying she believes we "must attack today's terrorists and the next generation's terrorists," she also says, "Our current strategy is not sustainable" and "we should use war as the last option, always and only for defense."

Given her understanding of economics and the role our current military spending plays in driving the national debt to record heights, we might have expected more. As an example, this year's military budget alone could cover almost the entire 10-year projected cost of the contentious health bill without putting us further and further into debt. Then again, since virtually none of the politicians or candidates from either the Democrat or Republican parties are offering specifics about cutting military spending, perhaps Otjen will sadly just blend in with the chorus of silence on this most important issue.

There are, however, some very significant issues on which she is less obtuse. Take the environment, for instance. Otjen calls herself "a Teddy Roosevelt Republican" and puts environmental protection as a high priority in her platform. She has already been endorsed by the national Republicans for Environmental Protection and Republicans United. The contrast with Rehberg, at least in this regard, could not be more stark.

Like all too many Republicans, Rehberg talks about "what's good for Montana." But his horrible record on the environment, one of the worst in Congress, belies his statements. When it comes to a choice between the economy and the environment, Rehberg doesn't hesitate to toss the environment overboard at the first chance. Otjen, however, believes that "environmental protection is not at odds with economic development. I believe that you do both together."

As her website notes: "Thirty years from now, we want a Montana where we all gather around the Thanksgiving family dinner table and enjoy fresh vegetables and meats from the farm or ranch right down the road. Our water is clean and crystal clear. Our view of the mountains is through the bluest sky." Little of that will be possible if Montana and the nation continue on their destructive path of coal mining and burning, but one thing is certain—she's not mouthing the standard Republican talking points.

Or how about abortion rights? Again, Otjen veers widely from the well-trod Republican path with her stance on a woman's right to choose, but does it under the rubric of individual privacy. "I have a right to my own bedroom and my body," she writes on her website. "Republicans must be consistent on this issue and make individual rights the guiding force on all public policy issues."

Although Otjen calls herself "a real Republican," it's hard to say how that will fly in a Montana Republican primary. If, as the National Republican Party seems to want, they coalesce in defiance to all things Democratic, as the "Party of No," then Otjen will likely fail in her primary bid. If, on the other hand, people are fed up with the partisan stranglehold in Washington, she might just do okay, especially if you consider the unknown potential for crossover voters and the Tea Party effect.

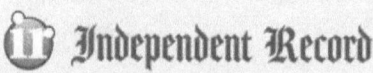

Billings Republican, A.J. Otjen, files for Congress

January 28, 2010 By CHARLES S. JOHNSON

A.J. Otjen, a self-described Teddy Roosevelt Republican, filed Tuesday to challenge five-term Republican Rep. Denny Rehberg for Montana's lone seat in the U.S. House.

Otjen, 52, is a political newcomer from Laurel who said she represents the state's moderate and independent voters.

Rehberg hasn't filed yet, but is already campaigning for re-election. Seeking the Democratic nomination in the June 8 primary are Tyler Gernant and Melinda Gopher, both of Missoula, and Dennis McDonald of Melville.

Otjen has been a business professor at Montana State University-Billings, teaching marketing since 2003. She previously owned Grand Canyon Airlines for six years and retired as vice president of marketing for Sprint Wireless Division in 2001.

"Denny has many old and loyal friends in Montana," Otjen said. "He is a good listener and storyteller. I admire that."

However, Otjen said Rehberg hasn't been able to pass into law any of the 25 bills he's sponsored this session of Congress, which began in January 2009. As a source, she cited the Web site, www.opencongress.org. The same Web site shows Democratic Sen. Jon Tester, D-Mont., passing none of the 16 bills and Democratic Sen. Max Baucus passing one of 25 bills they've sponsored since January 2009.

"The issues today are too serious for us not to send the very best representative possible," Otjen said. "Everything happening right now has consequences that impact how we will live in the future. It's time we stopped the ideology and started thinking about governing."

If elected, Otjen said her No. 1 goal is to balance the federal budget and boost the economy with a tax credit plan for small businesses." She called for protecting small businesses and launching sustainable strategies for the environment, energy, health and terrorism.

Otjen said Rehberg votes the Republican Party line 90 percent of the time and has been part of a Congress that hasn't balanced the budget in a decade.

Otjen called herself a centrist on social issues. She has said she supports a woman's right to abortion and gay and lesbian rights.

"Democrats don't have the answers either," she said. "As Will Rogers said, he did not belong to an organized party; he was a Democrat. They have vision but lack the ability to govern. We need two parties that work together for any chance at good government."

In response, Rehberg's campaign manager, Tyler Matthews, provided a list of legislation that the congressman has passed during his tenure, covering military issues, water projects, natural resources and post offices.

Matthews said, "Denny believes that new ideas and fresh faces are good for the political process, and he welcomes Ms. Otjen to the political process."

Matthews said Rehberg will continue working to make the federal government "more accountable to taxpayers and to bringing some fiscal discipline to Washington, D.C."

Comments:

I am interested in seeing how A.J. Otjen will do. The ultra-conservative Republicans, I feel, have made the Republican Party a very unwelcoming and unreachable party. When the moderates controlled the party, the party was more open and responsive to the public. In fact, the moderate Republicans were the first to fight for civil rights for minorities. Long before the Democrats even considered it. If I remember right, the Republicans passed civil rights laws as far back as the mid-1800s. But, the Dixiecrat Democrats reversed those laws quickly. And the Republican Party supported minorities in public offices from the very beginning.

The foundation of the Republican Party of conservative public policy and a compassionate government is sound. But, the party really lacks in being able to deliver that message to the right people at the right time. Too many inappropriate and inconsiderate comments by party leaders. A strong leader inspires a person to join their cause. I believe in conservative public policy. But, today's leaders really need to be more thoughtful of how their comments and how they approach certain issues. On election- day in 2008, I left the Republican Party because I was not going to listen one more time to an ultra-conservative Republican candidate or party leader make snide comment about American Indians in Montana.

Knowing our political history, I wouldn't really call it racism. It's just plain stupidity. And it is no longer acceptable in any public realm. Today, I don't believe these ultra conservatives remember the history of the Republican Party and it's reasoning for being. This is seriously the best news the Republican Party in Montana has had.
Fewer and fewer of we Montana Republicans are mouth-breathing, tea-bagging Birthers. Finally, some common-sense ideas from a Republican not beholden to the rabid right-wing special interested.

Will be fascinating to watch them devour themselves like the teabaggers are doing.

BILLINGS GAZETTE

Guest opinion: Small businesses need cash to boost the economy

January 09, 2010 By A.J. OTJEN

Financial institutions cut back on loans in the $101,000-to-$250,000 range by more than 60 percent in 2008. The massive removal of approximately $72 billion from the small-business credit market undoubtedly had an impact on almost 20 percent of small businesses folding in 2008. Statistics reflect the impact on small-business loans:

• Loans of $100,000 or less. In 2004, 13,580,000 loans made totaling $125.3 billion. In 2008, there were 10,261,105 loans made totaling $114.5 billion.

• Loans of $101,000 to 250,000. In 2004, 14,450,000 loans made totaling $228.4 billion. In 2008, there were 241,713 loans made totaling $42.5 billion.

In good years, small businesses had to pay taxes on their earnings, giving up a big chunk of cash — cash that could have sustained them now, or been used to invest in growth and jobs.

It would be better for the economy if we skipped a step (taxes and government) and let businesses put their cash directly in the banks, so that banks met their reserve requirement and were able to start lending (i.e. creating) money in the credit market.

The most feasible plan is a form of some Roth-like retaining-earnings tax category. Taxes would be paid forward. The maximum amount retained would reflect a "reasonable" expectation of profit generation in any one year. "Reasonable" can be defined as equal to one year of industry segment profitability (as averaged over the last 5 years) or $250,000, whichever is greater. This is reasonable because:

• The purpose of these retained earnings is to provide businesses with cash in off years.

• A major purpose of the "accumulated earnings tax" is to prevent retained earnings from being used as a tax loophole.

• Distribution from the retained earnings fund must be reported either as a direct business expense, thus nontaxable, or as a distribution (taxable on the interest earned).

Financial institutions may balk at providing a means by which small businesses can accumulate operational funds without the need for high-interest loans. While these small businesses' retained earnings funds would not interfere with the banks making loans or providing lines of credit there would be undoubtedly a downward pressure on the interest rates chargeable by banks.

Financial institutions could be encouraged to support a Roth-like small-business retained-earning fund because they could develop new products for the investment of this money. Also, administrative fees could be charged for providing oversight of these retained funds; and this cash on hand would help banks meet their reserve requirement for them to lend more money.

Making cash available to small businesses is essential to boosting our economy. First, we have got to grow ourselves out of our debt. Second, we have got to balance the budget. In addition to controlling spending, we have to find more revenues to balance the budget and that means creating new taxpayers with new jobs and economic growth.

A.J. Otjen of Laurel teaches university business courses and has announced her candidacy in the Republican primary for the U.S. House seat held by Denny Rehberg.

2009

 BILLINGS GAZETTE

3 steps to reducing costs of health care

November 22, 2009 By A.J.OTJEN

We spend over $2.5 trillion a year on health care. To reduce these costs by one-third we must:

1. Have a free market in the health care industry. The 85 percent of us with insurance do not see prices. We just ask, "is this covered?" Competition for MRIs or X-rays, etc., would make these costs go down.

2. Provide for private and some public incentives, innovation and investment in healthy lifestyles for individuals and communities. This means bike paths, inner-city vegetable gardens, recess and P.E. in our school systems and less saturated fats and high-fructose corn syrup in our food supply. Chronic disease is estimated to be 75 percent of the cost of our health care, primarily in those over age 45.

3. Invest in technology allowing for collection and payment, so that we see the prices first and stay within our own budget. This requires individual responsibility and an overall collective fund big enough to provide for catastrophic emergencies and universal care for all. It could be privately held or publicly held. This would reduce administrative costs, estimated at 31 percent of our health care.

Real leadership is more than tort reform or calling names like "The Pelosi Bill" or reading page numbers to make people angry too late in the process. Now we have a bill passed in the House that does nothing to lower costs or give us the health reform we really need.

BILLINGS GAZETTE

Guest opinion: Take Teddy Roosevelt Republicans off endangered-species list

October 24, 2009 By A.J. OTJEN

Montana's Teddy Roosevelt Republicans are not endangered. We may have been hibernating, but watch out now that we are waking up. It is time that we stop leaving the party to which we have been dedicated to our entire lives. Instead we should own it and take it back.

Republicans that have left because of the last decade of angry rhetoric and the far-right divisive politics and wedge issues must come back. Many Democrats, disenfranchised from their party, must come over. Together, we can create a movement to hold our politicians accountable to their constituents, something long absent from our political system. My heart has always been Republican even though in the last several years it has been broken. I refuse to leave. Many right-wing Republicans have asked me to get out. But it's not just about me. It's about all the voices who need to be heard.

The response to one voice standing up starts a ripple effect. There are hundreds of progressive Republican blogs. There are millions of real Republicans. We call ourselves Teddy Roosevelt Republicans. Though the dancing video with Teddy is fun to get attention, his speech about radicals and extremists that follows is as serious today as it was when he made it.

Reagan philosophy

Don't separate us from Ronald Reagan who said: "As to the issues that draw on the deep springs of morality and emotion, let us decide that we can disagree among ourselves as Republicans and tolerate the disagreement." He said that we should emphasize the things that unite us. Reagan would never tell someone to get out of the party. He said: "The person who agrees with you 80 percent of the time is a friend and an ally - not a 20 percent traitor."

Republicans have abandoned the concept of fiscal discipline. Teddy Roosevelt Republicans will stand up for it again. We must balance the budget. It is unrealistic to say spend less when our own Republicans have been spending more without paying for it. Taxing less is not going to balance the budget. I believe we need to safeguard the middle class and small business from tax increases whenever and wherever possible. Small business and the middle class are the job engine that will create 90 percent of all job growth in our economy.

Balance the budget

We must have more revenues in order to balance the budget. A "1 percent tax" would balance the budget. This means taking the top 1 percent of our excellent achievers up to a higher income tax of no more than 40 percent if it is necessary. For most of Reagan's two terms, this rate was 50 percent. My position is clearly Republican on this issue. I applaud these folks ability to get the most out of our infrastructure, but I also believe it means they are most responsible for maintaining it. The inherent flaw in modern conservatism is the idea that you can keep cutting taxes and that we will spend our economy out of a recession and out of debt all the while having complete and irresponsible disregard for the resulting deficit.

Republicans should develop a stimulus package to grow the economy to help reduce the debt. Obama's stimulus included misguided Democratic jobless waste. I believe in a sophisticated public infrastructure for this country that supports commerce and education. We should only go into long-term debt for long-term investment that sustains growth.

Both party extremes have failed. It is time for a strong centrist to stand for neither the left nor the right but push this economy up. We can no longer appease the leadership in either party but must present the alternative by electing the alternative. The TR Republicans are not on life support. We are back, and as tough as the grizzly bear. Let's get the best people back into politics so it can work again for both parties, and thus for the country.

A.J. Otjen of Laurel has taught in the Montana State University Billings College of Business for six years after working in the marketing field for 25 years and holds a doctoral degree in interdisciplinary social sciences (economics, history, political science and sociology). She has announced her candidacy as a Republican challenger to U.S. Rep. Denny Rehberg in the June 2010 primary election.

Response:

Not all who claim to be Republicans really are

November 02, 2009

As a Ronald Reagan conservative (and former state senator and former GOP state chairman), I have many issues with the Horse Sense column published on Oct.18. First of all, a political party should not be defined by a few of its elected officials but rather its platform. I would agree that a person can be a Republican and not be in lock step on every issue, but when your ideals generally lineup with one party over the other on nearly every issue, then that defines what party you are. Otherwise you're not being truthful with the electorate. Ms. Otjen's platform of higher government spending, redistribution of wealth through "progressive taxes", weakened military, stronger government controlled schools, fewer freedoms, no compassion for unborn babies or reverence for traditional marriage. Ms. Otjen is a Democrat.

Speaking of not being truthful with the electorate, John Bohlinger is a Democrat. He filed and ran as a Democrat for lieutenant governor. If he truly believes he is a Republican, then he should resign as lieutenant governor for perjuring himself on the candidate filing papers to run for that office and then truly run as a Republican.

I know many Montana Republicans and none of them want a polluted environment. We are all environmentalists. The difference is we want common sense regulations that protect the environment and Montana jobs. Harrison Fagg is a Republican and should not be compared to Ms. Otjen or the lieutenant governor.

Ken Miller

Laurel

BILLINGS GAZETTE

Horse sense: Otjen likely to conflict with state's Reagan Republicans

October 18, 2009 By CHARLES S. JOHNSON

HELENA - A.J. Otjen, an accomplished businesswoman and professor, recently declared that she intends to run as a "Teddy Roosevelt Republican" against U.S. Rep. Denny Rehberg in the June 2010 GOP primary.

Trouble is, "Teddy Roosevelt Republicans" are practically an extinct, or at least endangered, species in the Montana Republican Party.

You probably could stuff Montana's Teddy Roosevelt Republican elected officials into a phone booth and have room to spare.

Otjen's positions in support of abortion rights, gay marriage, a higher top federal income tax rate, Keynesian economics and U.S. withdrawal from Iraq and Afghanistan are clearly out of step with at least most elected Republicans in Montana.

Of course, anyone who meets the legal qualifications and pays the filing fee is free to run for office.

Otjen, who teaches marketing at Montana State University Billings, no doubt will devise a creative strategy to take on the five-term congressman. Her Web site has a fun video with mug shots of Roosevelt and her attached to a couple dancing the Charleston.

But in Montana, it is the Ronald Reagan Republicans who dominate the party. They sprang from the Goldwater Republicans in 1964.

Montanans who backed Reagan for the first time in 1980 were considered Ronnie-come-latelies. The hard-core Montana GOP establishment's support for him goes back to 1968 or at least 1976 when Reagan unsuccessfully challenged Republican President Gerald Ford.

Over the years moderate Montana Republicans have not always been welcomed in the GOP. Some Republican busybody purists go around branding moderates as RHINOs - Republican in name only. Among those so tagged was popular Gov. Marc Racicot, later chairman of the Republican National Committee.

Should any very moderate Republican get elected, they are often targeted with primary challenges or given the cold shoulder. Most eventually wind up drifting to the Democratic Party or dropping out.

Those Democrats who are not pro-choice or supported a sales tax know the feeling.

That's too bad. I've always believed in the "big tent" theory for both major political parties. There should be plenty of room under a party's circus tent to accommodate all degrees of views, so long as people generally agree on a few core principles.

There was a time long ago Montana Republicans embraced progressives.

One was Jeannette Rankin, who in 1916 became the first woman elected to Congress.

Another was Joe Dixon, rated by historians as Montana's best governor. He was elected governor in 1920 after stints in the U.S. House and Senate. Dixon was national campaign manager of Teddy Roosevelt's unsuccessful candidacy for president in 1912 on the Progressive or Bull Moose ticket.

But that was then.

In the early 1970s, some Republican legislators were made to feel unwelcome in their own House caucus because of their strong pro-environmental beliefs.

That led former Missoula Mayor George Turman to switch parties. He went on to be elected as a Democrat to the Public Service Commission and as lieutenant governor.

Another was Rep. Hal Harper of Helena, who lost in a Republican primary, switched parties and won his seat back. Harper served in the House for several decades, including as speaker. He is now Democratic Gov. Brian Schweitzer's chief policy adviser.

"There's no question that a bunch of us and more in the caucus knew how important our natural resources, including our animal and especially big game heritage, is to Montana," Harper said. "We could not see a Montana separated from that wonderful heritage that the Creator endowed us with into the future."

Another was Harrison Fagg of Billings, an avid hiker with strong views about protecting Montana's natural resources. He was knocked out in a primary in 1984 by a young Republican who then went by Dennis Rehberg.

Then there is John Bohlinger, a Billings businessman who served in the Montana House and Senate as a moderate Republican. He's now lieutenant governor with Schweitzer; they won as a cross-party team in 2004 and 2008.

"I'm still a Republican," Bohlinger said, "There are people in leadership who would like to expel me. I think we need to find common ground."

Bohlinger said he admires Roosevelt as a conservationist who understood the value of protecting the environment and as a trust-buster who stood up to corporations when they had excessive influence.

50

"There's got to be some Teddy Roosevelt Republicans out there beside myself, some moderates that want to accomplish the goals that I did," he said.

As for Otjen, Bohlinger said he is glad she's here in Montana.

Not by coincidence, hanging from the wall of Bohlinger's office in the Capitol is a huge mounted head of a bull moose, the very symbol of Teddy Roosevelt and his third-party candidacy.

The Billings Outpost

Challenger makes case to Republicans

October 15, 2009 By JENNIFER MOLK (paraphrased)

To a meeting of Republicans Otjen said, "Teddy Roosevelt was a Republican who focused on capitalism, conservatism and equal rights," which were also her principal beliefs.

She said, "I think I can start a movement to bring the party back to the middle. And then asked the group to "envision what they would like the world to look like. Technology can make our lives look like a Terminator movie or a world where we can sit down with our family for dinner and be eating clean food and drinking clean water. Our food came from the farmer down the street, the sky is blue and the city has a bike path from downtown to the suburbs. And the football game is on a big TV that is hanging in the air. The decisions we make today will determine which future we have."

On the economy, "I believe democracy has improved capitalism …because we vote to put in rules and regulations that make it better for the good of society."

She said she supported investing in infrastructure as commerce depended on it. She also said she could not vote for George W. Bush a second time because of the Bush Doctrine. She said, "The most powerful country in the world cannot strike first. It breaks everything we stand for. Is it moral to strike first, how can we claim to be the moral country and the moral party?

Hip Hop Republican.com did an interview with A.J. Otjen, a self-styled Teddy Roosevelt Republican running for Congress in Montana. Below is their interview.

A.J. Otjen: Progressive Republican for Congress

by Dennis Sanders on October 2, 2009

HHR Blog: Tell the readers of HHR Blog a little about yourself... where are you from... where were you born... where were you raised?

A.J. Otjen: I was raised in Enid Oklahoma by a Republican family. My grandfather William John Otjen was the Republican candidate for governor and senator for Oklahoma. I remember wearing "I like Ike" buttons as a small child and my mother being a "Bellmon Bell". My parents were divorced when I was 15. I think Mom was my hero as she paid for all of my college but always told me I was on my own the day I graduated and she meant it. She had the greatest friends that had parties and played bridge. The day she died I was able to tell her that she had been the best mom. That is all she wanted to know. That she could be proud of what she left behind. She also gave me a love of horses and a belief that I could do anything I wanted. Her name was Eva and I am named after her mother Agnes.

HHR Blog: How have your feelings about the City and the State you currently live in influenced you're, decision to run for office?

A.J. Otjen: The job I have of teaching has influenced me quite a bit. My students seem to ask me my opinions and what they think their future will be like. And Montana has such an incredible environment and so many resources that should be used to the benefit of all of us. The fact that we live in such a transformative age is staring me in the face and the current Republicans are not saying the right things or having the right influence. But I'm getting started a bit late. I fortunately have had deep principles developed over a long time, and just need to apply a few details to them.

HHR Blog: What is your current job and what are your duties in the current job you hold?

A.J. Otjen: I'm on the faculty of marketing at the college of business at Montana State University in Billings. I teach people how to make a profit in a market economy. I did it for 25 years, successfully. Then I retired to become a professor in God's country. I worked in agriculture, technology, sports, tourism, real estate, the marketing of those things. And now I have horse property. I understand the limits of water and pastureland. I think this should all be of benefit to Montana.

HHR Blog: What type of family were you raised in, and how has your upbringing shaped your political views?

A.J. Otjen: I grew up in a typical middle class difficult family. I made my own living immediately after graduating with a bachelors and paid for my own MBA at night, and eventually made it to the VP level of a fortune 500 company. I was the head of a household, and currently support myself successfully. As a woman this shaped my political views from conservative to moderate to progressive moderate. I would say that my parents were upper class in their child hoods or had upper class manners. But had middle class values. Two wars did that to them. I have extremely liberal views when it comes to human rights.

HHR Blog: Where did you attend College and what was the highest degree you attained?

A.J. Otjen: I have two graduate degrees or a terminal degree (doctorate). I attended Mizzou, University of Colorado for the MBA and back to University of Missouri but in Kansas City for the Doctorate. I worked for Sprint Corporation at the time. The HQ was right across the street from the KC campus so I seemed silly not to cross the street at night to study and go to class. It was writing the dissertation that was the hard part. I had been writing memos and emails for many years by then.

HHR Blog: What were your experiences like as a College Student compared to your experiences as a Professional in the work-place?

A.J. Otjen: I must confess it is easier to write an email than a term paper. And two of my degrees were earned before the invention of personal computers. The doctorate was much easier thanks to Microsoft. But I love the smell of a campus. I think it is the green grass. And great corporate moments are fleeting. Plus I love to sleep in late. But doing the job in real life is more fun than learning it in the classroom. I think that is why I try to give my student as much actual experience now that I teach. It took years to reach a level where I was experienced enough to be a good manager of people in the corporate world, where it took about three years to be a good teacher....granted after 25 years of working. Still, now that I'm a professor, there are times when I wish I could just pick the students I want to teach like I could pick the employees I wanted to manage. Unfortunately it doesn't work that way.

HHR Blog: If you have traveled throughout the United States, please share with our readers what you were able to ascertain about the various cultures of The United States?

A.J. Otjen: I traveled the best way, working for the Potato Farmers of America, having them show me the land and the best historical sites in the area. Food and music is usually the best way to experience the local culture. The best part about New York City, besides the theatre, is its different neighborhoods from Harlem to China Town. The South has the Cajun dancing and food, and architecture, Savannah and Charleston, and Jazz Jazz Jazz. I prefer the Gulf to the Atlantic in terms of the breeze. I like Main's lobster the best. And Pennsylvania's farm land is about the prettiest in the country. In Colorado, a hidden jewel is the San Luis Valley soaked in sunlight and brisk air and hardly a soul, where there is the international crowd in Vail just a hundred miles away. If you really want to understand America, you need to meet our natives from the SW to Montana to Seattle and listen to the drums. I have friends on the east coast who have gone to Europe several times but have never seen our American west. As for California, head north. No offense LA. But those trees will make you cry.

HHR Blog: How do the various cultures of The United States compare to the dominant cultures in your home state?

A.J. Otjen: Many in Montana think you have to be born here. It is not true. Just like in all America. We are all immigrants. I'm a daughter of the American Revolution... And a first family of Virginia.... My nephew just married a Cherokee/Choctaw and I say it is about time we had some Oklahoma native blood in our family after having been part of the family that helped bring that state into the union. NUTZ I say.

Cherokee and Choctaw are from Florida and North Carolina and part of the Five Civilized Tribes. We are all immigrants. Talk to the Crow and Cheyenne in terms of who belongs to Montana. The more we all mix it up the more beauty I see in our skin and hair and healthy figures. Maybe the dominant culture in Montana is farmers and ranchers. But there are Germans, and French, and natives and Mormons that settled this land. There is big money and poverty. I don't think anyone dominates here anymore. We all want good things for each other if we think about it.

HHR Blog: What do you like the most about The United States?

A.J. Otjen: The constitution. The land. The history. The sacrifices made to get to where we are today. The potential of our future. The bravery of most of its citizens.

HHR Blog: What would you like to change the most about The United States and how would you accomplish this goal?

A.J. Otjen: I want to change the ugly rhetoric. I want the populace to be educated with the truth. I want the populace to be healthy. I want our economy based on green energy and technology that makes us more healthy and educated. I want information available to the entire world that is honest.

HHR Blog: What attracted you to your current political party? Did some occurrence in your life influence you in your choice of your current party affiliation?

A.J. Otjen: Yes, it was a part of my family when I was very young. Teddy was great. And now I want it to be good again. It makes me mad that everyone says there are no smart Republicans. It makes me mad that there are so many that make us look like fools.

HHR Blog: If you served in the Military which branch of the military did you serve in, and how has this shaped your views as a politician?

A.J. Otjen: No but my grandfather and father and uncles and nephew served in the army proudly, in combat. As a politician, it makes me want to stand up and fight for the constitution and not let fear tactics work in our politics. We are a brave nation. How dare we give up any of our rights in the name of fear of terror? Too many have died to protect our rights.

HHR Blog: What does your political agenda for both your constituency as well as the Nation consists of?

A.J. Otjen: I go into most of it on my website.

HHR Blog: What are your views on Gay Marriage?

A.J. Otjen: I am for it. I have many gay friends who deserve to be happy and have been together for a long time. I do not judge people based on their sex lives and I don't understand people who do. I believe that all people have a right to privacy and a right to pursue happiness. If I have a right to marriage than everyone does. In fact, Republicans should agree on this issue as something with which the government should not interfere as it is our creed to protect individual rights.

HHR Blog: What are your views on abortion?

A.J. Otjen: I believe that a woman is a human that is being, a human being, and that she is the one with the right to privacy. The unborn is dependent on the mother. The government has no right to intrude upon this woman's right. The best way to reduce the number of abortions is to prevent unwanted pregnancy in the first place.
In terms of third trimester medical terminations, I can't imagination that a pregnant mother wants to lose their child. It must be an incredible medical tragedy. A horrific situation. Has anyone ever known a mother that must lose their child in the third trimester, it is horrible. God bless the doctors still available to these poor mothers in those horrible private situations. Anyone who calls them killers is a disgrace.

HHR Blog: What are your beliefs and policies regarding Healthcare?

A.J. Otjen: The plan should work on health first. Such as taxing products or industries with high fructose corn syrup or saturated fats first. And then giving that money to support inner city vegetable gardens and back paths and more recess in school systems. Then I want to keep the health care providers in a free market where users can see the prices and shop around. Once they shop for MRIs as an example, they choose the cheapest. If the doctor says the hospital costs $5000 but the clinic down the street costs $500, then they should get their MRI down the street. Then they can pay their bill via a collective payment system that is a single payer system supported by the public.

HHR Blog: What are your views about the economy and effective ways to pull the United States out of the current recession it is in?

A.J. Otjen: Like Richard Nixon, I am a Keynesian. I believe in government spending us out of a crises. I explain this much more on my website. I also support tax cuts for middle class when possible. Income inequality is terrible for our economy.

HHR Blog: What do you think about the United States' involvement in both Iraq and Afghanistan?

A.J. Otjen: I want to get us out of Iraq and Afghanistan and go after criminal with intelligence and law enforcement and allies. I only want to be in a war as a defense, not offense.

HHR Blog: What are your policies concerning housing, financial assistance, and education for the low-income poor of the United States?

A.J. Otjen: The problem with capitalism is that it concentrates where there is profit. The result is tha there is little investment in the low income areas because there is little profit in these areas. Jack Kemp had a good idea about enterprise zones. Not everything is profitable and we have to support a public good as a result. We need to find a way to get a good return on investment in these areas. For everyone involved. People need to be able to buy a home, enjoy property gains, own businesses, educate children. How do we end the cycle: is it drugs and health that prevents a return on investment? The native Americans have said they need their own banking system. Maybe that would make a difference.

HHR Blog: What do you believe to be the future of education for our Nation's children and our youth (18-22 yrs. Old)?

A.J. Otjen: It must be great. We have to get it there. We have no option. I am for an expansion of public education. I am a professor. And I am against performance pay for teachers. I don't want teachers to compete against each other and there is not a good way to evaluate them.

A.J. Otjen: I see myself back as a professor. I am hoping to start a movement for younger progressives proving that we can win.

HHR Blog: If you were to run for President of the United States who would your ideal running mate be and why?

A.J. Otjen: One of you. Somebody young.

HHR Blog: Finally, Why do you call yourself a Progressive Republican? Is not progressivism an ideology more in line with the Democrat Party?

A.J. Otjen: No, look at Teddy. And Democrats are not very good at getting things done with the government in terms of the budget. They are good at passing social law issues but they usually mess up the end game.

HHR Blog: Who is your favorite Republican President and why?

A.J. Otjen: Teddy....saw the future of capitalism and tried to fix it and loved our national parks

HHR Blog: You voted for Barack Obama for President why did you do this?

A.J. Otjen: I think he is the right man for the right time. He has vision, he seems honest. And I think he will make the world resoect us again. I trust him with our foreign policy.

HHR Blog: Are there things in which you disagree with President Obama on?

A.J. Otjen: I am not sure anyone quite understands the banking finance issue. I have lots of degrees on this and I can't quite get what he is doing. I thought we should have input more cash instead of more credit into the market. And I don't get what any of them are doing on the health care plan. But we should give him a chance, it is early. I believe in a loyal opposition. And our Republican leaders are being really silly.

HHR Blog: We wish you much success in your campaign it was a pleasure. Thanks for sitting down with HipHopRepublican.com

Comments:

I don't think she's going anywhere. And it's a good thing.

Wait…I thought this was a Republican site? Everything I read seems right out of Media Matters and Moveon.org.

Let me see if I get this right. You seem to be supporting Otjen. She says above:

This fool works in the *school of business*?

To be blunt, Otjen is what's wrong with the country and what's wrong with the Republican Party. She is not a Republican in any way shape or form.

BILLINGS GAZETTE

Market doesn't work for health insurance

September 27, 2009 By A.J.OTJEN

First, why doesn't the health reform include a high tax on anything made with a lot of high fructose corn syrup and saturated fats, and that revenue then given to the school system to pay for more recess and P.E., inner city bike paths and vegetable gardens?

Second, the big health care cost is profit. I teach people how to make a profit in a market economy so I'm all for profit. But maybe not in this industry - as profit is not adding value here. The free market is not working as the customer cannot see the price. I think the private insurance industry does not work and does not add value. Let the doctors and hospitals stay in a free market system and compete to lower costs and increase quality, but the customers must see the prices for it to work.

We can send our bills to a single payer or public option, some kind of collection and payment system, which should be about 15 percent of our GDP or $2 trillion. We're paying more than that now with insurance benefits, so I have no problem transferring that to paying it in taxes to a collective system if it is as efficient as the post office. It is time to change the entire paradigm. Healthcare would not be socialized. Only the payment system would be - sort of like Paypal on the Internet.

www.ingramcontent.com/pod-product-compliance
Lightning Source LLC
Chambersburg PA
CBHW050514290526
45786CB00007B/2556